RECONSTRUCTING PSYCHOLOGICAL PRACTICE

Reconstructing Psychological Practice

Edited by
Ian McPherson and Andrew Sutton

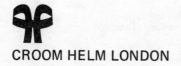

CROOM HELM LONDON

8939

© 1981 Ian McPherson and Andrew Sutton
Croom Helm Ltd, 2–10 St John's Road, London SW11

British Library Cataloguing in Publication Data

Reconstructing psychological practice
   1. Psychology
   I. McPherson, Ian
   II. Sutton, Andrew
   150   BF121

ISBN 0-7099-0419-3
ISBN 0-7099-1709-0 Pbk

Printed and bound in Great Britain by
Biddles Ltd, Guildford and King's Lynn

CONTENTS

Tempora mutantur, et nos mutamur in illis

PREFACE

This book concerns the present dilemmas and foreseeable problems of 'psychological practice', which in this context refers to the direct provision of psychological services to individual clients or client groups. Its contributors argue the need for major changes in how these services are delivered, their words being addressed as much to the users of psychology as to their fellow psychologists.

Psychological practice in Britain is largely a provision within the public service, shared between the National Health Service (clinical psychologists in psychiatric hospitals and certain other settings), local government (educational psychologists in local education authorities, and a growing involvement by psychologists of all kinds in social services departments) and in the penal service. These divisions have at times led to considerable parochialism, isolation and even antipathy between psychologists, a state of anomie in which it can be hard to discern features common to all psychological practice. The contributors to this book represent practice in health, education and welfare at a variety of levels. Their responses to the problems of practice are individual ones, formulated in diverse professional backgrounds, and their presentations reflect their diverse personal styles. Their common feature is that they are all known to be 'advanced' (or at least different) in their views about how psychology should be practised.

Economic recession is the harsh reality behind the issues to be discussed here, for psychological practice must increasingly face demands for effectiveness and cost-effectiveness. Educational psychology, the longest established and largest branch of psychological practice, is already facing problems of widespread graduate unemployment and a cutting back of establishments. The editors are keenly aware that talk of 'restructuring' at this time might prove a two-edged sword, with deleterious effects for some practitioners. This book, however, is directed primarily to the welfare of clients and potential clients, and to this goal we hope that it will be read not only by psychologists (and would-be psychologists) but also by those in other fields whose work might benefit from a changed psychological practice. We hope that those who disagree with the formulations and suggestions made here will say so, and advance their own. We do not claim to predict the future of psychological practice, we certainly do not

9

prescribe it. But that future might have to be very different from the immediate past, and sooner than many of us might comfortably prefer.

Ian McPherson
Andrew Sutton

1 THE DILEMMA OF CLINICAL PRACTICE: SURVIVING AS A CLINICAL PSYCHOLOGIST

David Hawks

Clinical psychologists, though they are not alone in this, confront a peculiar dilemma. If they acknowledge the nature of the problems which present themselves to them they must concede the paucity of their role in intervening in them. Faced with such a dilemma, clinical psychologists have reacted in a variety of ways. It is to a definition of these ways and an examination of the alternatives that this chapter is devoted.

The Nature of the Condition

The problems with which clinical psychologists are faced in their clinical practice are rarely simple unidimensional conditions. At the very least they will almost certainly have existed for some time and will, in addition to their disabling effects, serve important functions which are not easily replaced; they will also involve others. They will in part owe their origin to developmental processes embedded in the person's history and also reflect contemporary circumstances. Treatment, if it is to be successful, will have to identify some of these functions, discern some of the important reinforcements and recognise some of the important contributing circumstances. In other words, it will need to reflect some of the complexity of the condition itself. It is unlikely that there will be available to clinical psychology the equivalent of 'broad band antibiotics' effective across a wide variety of conditions. Confronted with this complexity and the need to reflect it in their practice, clinical psychologists face a dilemma. If they pursue the implications of this insight, it will be obvious, indeed it can readily be demonstrated, that the number of cases that they can deal with is infinitesimal in relation to the number which present themselves (Hall, 1970; Hawks, 1971; Lickorish and Sims, 1971).

11

The Nature of the Present Response

Denial

Clinical psychologists exhibit a number of strategies for dealing with this dilemma. Some have circumscribed their practice and redefined the problem. Others have accepted the situation as defined, but denied its problematic nature. It must be assumed for example that psychoanalysts, when recommending a course of analysis involving weekly attendance over a period of *x* years do not concern themselves with the economy of such a recommendation, or its inevitable exclusiveness. A less extreme response has been to accept the situation as it presently is but to argue the need for additional practitioners (British Psychological Society, 1973), thus making the assumption that the number of practitioners can conceivably match the demand for their services, an assumption which even in less parlous times is unlikely to be fulfilled.

Another response, while not denying the complexity of the problems or the need to reflect their complexity in the treatments offered, denies their pervasiveness. Such an approach accepts the definition of prevalence reflected in hospital statistics or psychiatric out-patient attendances. If there are 300 new admissions a year to a particular psychiatric hospital and 12,000 new out-patient attenders, it is possible to calculate the number of practitioners required to treat these cases assuming optimal or minimal criteria. If fewer practitioners are presently available, the obvious solution is to increase their number. If such an approach is not to yield answers which even its proponents cannot countenance, it must exclude from its calculations the indications of psychiatric morbidity in the community (Shepherd *et al.*, 1966; Goldberg and Blackwell, 1970; Brown and Harris, 1978) and the evidence that referral to psychiatric facilities is frequently a haphazard process which in no way reflects the severity of conditions or the likely efficacy of the means employed to treat them (Srole *et al.*, 1962; Mishler and Waxler, 1963; Scheff, 1966; Dohrenwend and Crandell, 1970; Wing and Hailey, 1972). In other words, for such an approach to 'work' requires that its advocates accept the present structure of services whose scarcity and admission policies determines, rather than reflects, the numbers of patients presenting for such services. It requires that its practitioners accept that definition of their 'case-load' as follows from the assumption that those people who need their services are those who are referred to them. That too few patients will thereby benefit is answered by calling for more practitioners rather than by any more radical rethinking of the nature of the required response.

Over-simplification

Quite another response to the dilemma depicted at the beginning of this chapter is to deny that the majority of problems presented to clinical psychologists are complex and to adopt a symptomatic, ahistorical approach to the understanding of disorder, from which it follows that a mechanistic, if not automated approach to their assessment and treatment can be recommended (Miller, 1968; Peck and Gathercole, 1968). Even if it is allowed that there are some so-called simple conditions permitting of simple solutions, even their number is such as to overwhelm the present availability of resources (Agras *et al.*, 1969; Marks, 1970; 1973; Bryant *et al.*, 1976).

Changed Venue of Practice

One wholly unrealistic solution to the dilemma has been to change the venue of psychological practice. If, it is argued, the majority of those having psychological problems never consult psychiatrists or are admitted to psychiatric hospital, or if they are admitted, do so when their problems are so long-standing as to be extremely difficult to treat, the answer is to make psychological services available at a primary-care level, notably by attaching clinical psychologists to general practices and social services departments (Broadhurst, 1972; Bender, 1972; 1979a; McAllister and Philip, 1975; Johnston, 1978). Better still, it is argued, the insights of clinical psychology should be available to the whole of medicine and not just psychiatry, from which it follows that psychologists should be attached to the various clinical departments of general hospitals not, as has been the case in the past, just to departments of psychiatry (Hetherington, 1967). It is not necessary to deny the desirability of this development in order to demonstrate its impracticability. If there have been too few clinical psychologists to meet the needs of the psychiatric services (British Psychological Society, 1973), then it is clearly unrealistic to imagine that there will be sufficient to meet the needs of medicine in general. The attachment of clinical psychologists to health centres, while an understandable expression of psychology's exploration of its role in relation to medicine, can never be other than an extravagant experiment which, while it may benefit those particular practices (and even this requires to be demonstrated), can hardly be the prescription for the future given the number of such centres. Given the impracticability of the proposal, the current tendency for clinical psychologists to seek attachments to health centres and social services departments can only be construed as part of an attempt to achieve independence of psychiatry; it cannot be regarded as a more rational deployment of their skills.

Advocacy of More Clinical Psychologists

Implicit in the discussion of several of the 'adjustments' dealt with above is the view that there never will be enough clinical psychologists. While this view may have a certain credibility in the present economic circumstances, there is nothing self-evident about it which recommends its uncritical acceptance. It must be rejected none the less, not on practical grounds, but on theoretical grounds. We simply cannot afford, in any sense, to allow psychiatric problems to occur making the assumption that there will be a sufficient number of psychologists to treat them, in the same way as it cannot be a solution to the built-in obsolescence of cars to provide a sufficient number of garages. The built-in obsolescence of cars is *itself* a problem which needs to be addressed in the same way as is the 'predictable' psychological disability of populations. The answer must surely be not more garages, but better cars; similarly the answer to human misery cannot be a prescription for more clinical psychologists, but better, that is, more competent human beings.

Given the complexity of human development and the probability of disabilities occurring, it is simply unrealistic to wait until problems arise and then refer them to clinical psychologists. In the same way it would be unrealistic if, in the face of widespread harmful educational practices, it was proposed that educational psychologists be employed to address the consequences of these practices. If clinical psychological practice (or educational psychological practice for that matter) as conventionally understood, involving as it does individual clients, is to make any sort of sense, the number of individuals requiring these services must be reduced. People must be enabled to cope better with the problems which inevitably arise in the course of life without recourse, except in rare instances, to psychologists.

Escape

One 'adjustment' shown by some clinical psychologists faced with the dilemma identified at the outset of this chapter is to leave the field altogether. The fact that many clinical psychologists resort to this solution — as attested by a number of surveys carried out in Britain (Kear-Colwell, 1972; White, 1972; Barden, 1979) — would itself recommend examination of the present structuring of psychological practice, even if there were no other causes, since it must be assumed that a majority of those leaving clinical practice do so because they are dissatisfied. Whatever the justification of such defection, it can hardly be argued that it constitutes a solution to the problems posed by clinical practice.

The Need for a New Response

Emphasis on Primary Prevention

If, as argued here, it is no solution to the problems posed to deny the complexity or pervasiveness of human misery, or to employ mechanistic methods of treatment or merely to change the venue of clinical practice, what stance must clinical psychologists take? The answer must surely be on the one hand to attempt to reduce the occurrence of problems in so far as this is possible, and on the other, in the event of their recurring, to enable people to cope better with them without extensive recourse to professional services. Both objectives are obviously capable of only partial realisation — what will be argued in the remaining parts of this chapter is that psychological practice and research must give much greater emphasis to their fulfilment.

It might be argued that nothing new is being advocated here. It has always made more sense to prevent the occurrence of illness, whether physical or psychological, than to attempt to treat it once it has arisen. Moreover, it is clear that the major advances made in the alleviation of physical illnesses have occurred as a result of preventive measures and the general improvement of man's living conditions, rather than the application of 'curative' medicine. Whatever may be the logic of the argument and the lessons of history, it is clear that clinical psychologists have not aligned their practice or their research activities accordingly. We still know extraordinarily little about the principles governing mental health, and when clinical psychologists have given advice regarding such matters that advice has often been contradictory, as evidenced by the controversies surrounding child-rearing practices. To point to the paucity of our knowledge in this area is not to deny the complexity of the issues, it is only to suggest that clinical psychologists have not yet invested sufficient importance in their resolution. Clinical psychologists have instead diverted themselves with further involvement in the intricacies of an ever-increasing repertoire of therapies, the application of which, even if they were effective, would be of little consequence to the vast majority of those suffering psychological disability.

Instead of displaying a growing preoccupation with the 'fine tuning' of Personal Construct Therapy, Gestalt Therapy, Transactional Analysis, Zen and Morita Therapy and Family Therapy, clinical psychologists should be concerned to see how they can give psychology away, how the insights psychology has achieved can be made available to the greatest number of people. In this connection it might be asked to what extent it is possible to define 'psychological first-aid'; a self-help kit of psychological techniques which will become as widely known and understood as the knowledge that burns should be held under cold water to reduce tissue temperature. Whatever the difficulty of discerning them, such psychological principles do exist — if they didn't even more people than at present would suffer psychological disabilities. The majority of children do not develop school phobia, the majority of housewives do not become agoraphobic or depressed, most people do cope with bereavement. Clinical psychologists, by investing themselves in the treatment of problems once they have arisen, have neglected the study of those circumstances in which they do not. The solution to the widespread malaise confronting clinical psychologists cannot be the employment of an ever-increasing proportion of the population in the provision of services to the remainder, it must be the discernment of those means whereby the majority of people cope with the problems which confront them and the promulgation of such means. Psychological services should be the final resort of people with problems, not the preferred and professionally promoted solution to these problems.

It might be argued that what is being required of clinical psychologists here is too onerous a task (the discernment of those principles of development which protect people against breakdown and, when breakdown occurs, enable them to cope) and that some limitation of their responsibility has to be accepted. While this point must be conceded, as psychologists cannot alone be made responsible for the exercise of benevolent government, the limitations in the definition of their role adopted by many clinical psychologists have amounted to professional myopia. Clinical psychologists have concerned themselves with the psychological dynamics of particular patients without enquiring about their life circumstances, or have seen patients in their consulting rooms without consideration of the wards from which they have come. So convinced have they been of their own therapeutic omnipotence, they have acted as if the interventions and insights achieved during the 'therapeutic hour' somehow outweighed the influence of the patient's other environments, however malevolent these may be. When the omnipotence of clinical psychologists has been punctured, as happens when patients fail to get well despite the psychologist's intervention, it is sometimes assumed that this is because patients are not motivated to following the psychologist's prescription, rather than that formulations, concentrating on patients *in vacuo*, are inevitably flawed.

When patients prepared for discharge cannot be discharged for want of accommodation in the community, or when patients' reinforcement regimes cannot be maintained in the ward because of the frequent turnover and absenteeism of nursing staff, the response called for is not for clinical psychologists to define such cases as untreatable, but to redefine the problems, that is to involve themselves in seeking alternative accommodation and to study the basis of nurse dissatisfaction. That clinical psychologists do not usually regard their responsibilities in this way is suggested by the fact that while there have been a number of enquiries into conditions inside psychiatric and subnormality hospitals, clinical psychologists have not been prominent in drawing attention to such conditions, despite the fact that most such hospitals have psychologists in post. One can only assume clinical psychologists did not notice such conditions, or if they noticed them, did not think it their responsibility to draw attention to them.

While accepting that clinical psychologists must accept limitations on their professional concern, if only to preserve their sanity, it might be argued that too often this limitation has amounted to negligence, even in areas of legitimate professional concern like the care afforded patients in psychiatric hospitals.

Individual Clinical Practice

What then are the implications of this viewpoint for individual and corporate psychological practice? To the extent that clinical psychologists feel it justified (or are required) to see individual patients — and it would seem to be necessary to do so if only to achieve a certain credibility as therapists — then their practice should reflect the complexity of the conditions treated. They should achieve some familiarity with the patient's 'life space', the significant others in their lives; they should, in so far as this is possible, involve these significant others (who need not be confined to the patient's immediate family) in the treatment of the patient; they should aspire to hand over responsibility for the patient as soon as possible; they should explain the basis of their intervention to the patient and to his or her significant others, they should 'give the medicine away'. They should regard the individual case as a manifestation of more general principles, the discernment of which is an important psychological task no less legitimate than the treatment of individuals. While responding to individuals with psychological problems will continue to be a necessary part of society's compassion, it is the more general promulgation of preventive measures which provides the only realistic response.

Corporate Clinical Practice

The views expressed here also have implications for the way clinical psychological practice is structured. Many clinical psychologists work in relative isolation and even those departments which have larger staffs tend to deploy psychologists very thinly, allocating perhaps one or two psychologists to work with the elderly, one or two to care for the mentally handicapped, etc. Given the scarcity of clinical psychologists and the unlikelihood of their numbers being significantly increased in the foreseeable future, it must be asked whether this practice is geared to the needs of the population, or even to the needs of the individual psychologists, who working in isolation and without the support of professional colleagues may become disillusioned, or else develop the myopia already alluded to.

What might make more sense would be for clinical psychologists, grouped in area or district departments with defined geographic responsibilities, to specify, if necessary by undertaking the required research, what are the most pressing needs for their service, to determine which of these are amenable to psychological intervention and to undertake such interventions with the aim of passing on the necessary skills to others in due course. If psychological practice was structured in this way it is likely that clinical psychologists would more often work in teams rather than as individuals with the benefit to morale which this would almost certainly confer. Resources would be concentrated in specific areas of application, objectives would more quickly be realised, or found to be unrealisable, problems could be tackled at various levels simultaneously. The style of work of clinical psychologists would be more akin to that of clinical researchers concerned with the application of their findings. While inevitably the grouping of psychologists advocated here would result in the withdrawal of some of the services presently being provided by clinical psycho-logists, particular projects when realised would be replaced by others. Priorities would not be statically defined, but subject to redefinition.

The penalty, if it might be called such, of this harbouring of resources would be the loss to individual clinical psychologists of the relative autonomy that they enjoy at present — their right to do as they please within the constraints imposed ultimately by district or area health authorities. The work of departments of clinical psychology would become more programmed, more subject to consultation within the department, less the manifestation by individual entrepreneurship.

It might be argued that the processes advocated here would merely result in departments continuing to do what they are already doing, that contemporary clinical psychological practice reflects just such an implicit process of consultation and definition of priorities. The evidence would appear to contradict such a view. Clinical psychologists are frequently in the situation of responding to the expectations of other professions rather than to a definition of what they consider they can most usefully do; their activities do not appear to reflect a consideration of priorities; they are often deployed across a wide spectrum of services with little prospect of significant change in any one of these spheres. Except with respect to individual patients, and we have already considered how impractical it is to concentrate exclusively on the individual, the circumstances in which problems manifest themselves, and the nature of society's response to them, will remain unchanged.

To be convinced of the advantages of the restructuring of practice advocated here, one need only consider the benefits of, for example, defining the resettlement in the community of those eligible persons presently in mental handicap hospitals as a departmental priority. Instead of only one or two psychologists being identified with this objective, a team of five or six might be engaged in this enterprise thus allowing the tasks of identifying suitable patients, locating suitable housing, training support staff and providing specialised advice with respect to particular patients to be addressed *simultaneously*. The activities of clinical psychologists would be more project orientated, having a defined objective, finite time scale and resources more adequate to the task. Such grouping of clinical psychologists would allow a complementation of skills and a degree of support usually lacking when clinical psychologists work in comparative isolation from one another. The objective of such projects would not necessarily be to perpetuate a service provided by clinical psychologists, but, having formulated a response, to ensure that this was implemented by others where appropriate.

Conclusions

It has been argued in this chapter that the relative scarcity of clinical
psychologists is only a problem when clinical psychological practice is
construed as providing a one-to-one therapeutic relationship. If it is
accepted that clinical psychologists can never provide such a service,
and it is questionable as to whether they should even attempt it, and
instead of demanding more and more clinical psychologists, consideration is given to redefining the clinical task, radical implications for the
individual and corporate practice of clinical psychology emerge.

Individual patients, if seen, should be seen in order that diagnostic
and therapeutic skills can be developed with a view to giving them
away and in order to reveal the working of more general principles of
psychopathology. To continue to see individual patients exclusively,
however, is not only to perpetuate a discriminatory activity, it is
clearly impracticable given the prevalence of psychological disorder.

Nor is it only individual clinical psychological practice which
warrants examination in the light of these premises. Much corporate
clinical psychological practice appears not to reflect any consideration
of priorities, whether of needs or of competence, but rather reflects
the expectations of other professions and the idiosyncratic preferences
of clinical psychologists. The price of this entrepreneurism would
seem, in many instances, to have been the disillusionment of staff who,
inadequate to the task they have set themselves or have been set by
others, have left the field or become cynical while continuing to
practice in it. Individual initiatives have flowered only to wither when
those initiating them depart. What would seem called for is much more
corporate consideration of objectives, more concentration of scarce
resources, offering the prospect of at least modest success.

2 CLINICAL PSYCHOLOGY IN PRIMARY HEALTH CARE: DEVELOPMENT OR DIVERSION?

Ian McPherson

Clinical psychologists have, if rather belatedly, begun to recognise that the vast majority of psychological problems for which people seek help are dealt with not by the specialist hospital-based services of the type clinical psychologists have traditionally operated but at a primary care level, and largely by general practitioners. Estimates of the actual prevalence rate of psychological problems in general practice vary considerably but Shepherd *et al.* (1966) in a major survey found a total prevalence rate of 14 per cent, making psychological disturbance the second most common cause of consultation for women and the fourth most common for men. Only one in twenty of all these cases was referred for specialist help. Such findings have led to the argument that primary care is a more appropriate level for clinical psychologists to deliver a service and over the past eight years numerous articles have been written and conferences held on the theme of clinical psychology and primary health care, reflecting the increasing interest and involvement of psychologists in this area.

Broadhurst (1972) was the first directly to suggest the possible contribution clinical psychologists might make to the work of the general practitioner, a more detailed argument for a closer liaison being put forward by Kincey (1974). It is of interest in the light of subsequent developments in this field that these early papers did not foresee the psychologist solely in a therapeutic role in primary health care. In 1973 a clinical psychologist was appointed to work on a full-time basis in general practice for the first time. This resulted in the first report of a psychologist's experience of actually working at this level (McAllister and Philip, 1975), which concluded that the psychologist had a useful role to play though it was acknowledged that there was a need to adapt to the demands of the new setting. A wider picture of clinical psychologists' involvement in general practice at this time comes from a survey of clinical psychologists in the United Kingdom carried out by Broadhurst (1977), from which it was estimated that one in seven psychologists were working with general practitioners. The majority of these were receiving direct referrals for individual treatment, usually only involving a small number of cases with the

21

patients mainly being seen in hospital-based departments. This survey indicated that psychologists' involvement with GPs was no longer a minority interest and that there was a desire among a substantial part of the profession to increase this contact. Official recognition and guarded approval of this development was given in the *Trethowan Report* (1977) on the role of psychologists in the health services and there is no sign at present that psychologists' enthusiasm for working in primary health care is waning, though some concern has been expressed as to the direction this involvement is taking (Hood, 1979; McPherson, 1980).

An important feature of this development is that it might require a major change in the way in which psychological services are organised. The view that establishing links between clinical psychologists and primary care should consist of more than just allowing direct referrals from GPs to hospital-based psychologists has gained considerable popularity, and it is suggested that psychologists should become members of the primary health care team. Arguments in favour of this tend to emphasise the possibilities of an improved service by psychologists as a result of earlier intervention closer to the patient's natural environment, together with greater continuity of care due to improved communication between the psychologist and other members of the primary health care team, as well as easier physical and psychological access for the patient with the accompanying reduction in stigma. While such ideas have considerable face validity, the apparent desire for a large-scale move into a new area with the likely consequences of an increased work-load for a profession which is generally considered to have insufficient manpower to meet existing commitments (e.g. Barden, 1979) seems to suggest altruism verging on masochism, or alternatively that there is more to this move than a desire to do good in the community. It does in fact appear likely that clinical psychologists have seen work in primary care as not just offering the satisfaction of operating an improved service, but also as offering a more attractive working environment, where their skills would receive greater recognition and where they might avoid the demarcation disputes and inter-professional rivalries that can arise in services based within the psychiatric system. This is not to suggest that what is beneficial for the profession is in some way incompatible with what is good for the service, indeed these factors may well interact such that psychologists working in a less restrictive setting would be able to function more effectively. Nevertheless it seems worthwhile going beyond what for some psychologists has become a self-evident assumption, that increased involvement by psychologists in primary health care is necessarily a good thing, and considering what are likely to be the main advantages of this development and for whom.

Advantages for Patients

All discussions of the benefits of clinical psychologists working in primary health care emphasise the large numbers of patients currently seeking help for psychological problems at this level. The fact, however, that high prevalence rates do not necessarily mean that psychologists would have a useful role is often overlooked. The value of the psychologist's contribution would depend on the nature of the problems, the effectiveness of the intervention, together with the appropriateness and practicality of such a service. To examine this question McPherson and Feldman (1977) carried out an investigation on a sample of patients presenting with psychological problems in two group practices. This study found support for the view that the psychological problems seen in general practice are of the type with which psychologists deal, but it identified another difficulty — that of how psychologists could respond to the vast source of potential referrals. McPherson and Feldman point out that impracticality of psychologists offering traditional individual therapy in this situation unless only for a small select group of patients, which would make questionable the advantages for patients as a whole of having a psychological service available at a primary health care level.

Other studies (e.g. McAllister and Philip, 1975; Johnston, 1978; Ives, 1979; Koch, 1979; Clark, 1979) have tended to focus more directly on the advantages for patients who do come into contact with psychologists both in terms of the effectiveness of therapy and of receiving it in a primary care setting rather than in a hospital. The majority of these studies have not been controlled evaluations but rather reviews of clinical work with some attempt to assess outcome, and the authors all point out the problems in drawing general conclusions from their findings because of the absence of basic methodological requirements for outcome research such as control groups, independent 'blind' evaluation, adequate follow-up, etc. Nevertheless, it is easy in briefly scanning the published literature to obtain the impression that primary care patients have a lot to gain from having access to clinical psychologists. It is rather sobering, therefore, to turn to a study by Earll and Kincey (1980) which is currently the only controlled evaluation of the effectiveness of a psychologist's intervention in this area. Referrals were randomly assigned either to treatment by a psychologist or to the continuation of their management by the

GP, and all patients were interviewed by a 'blind' assessor at follow-up. Subjective outcome was measured by three standardised self-administered questionnaires concerning psychological symptoms and life satisfaction. Earll and Kincey found that, while there was a high level of consumer satisfaction in that 85 per cent of patients felt that their contact with the psychologist had helped 'to some extent' or 'a great deal', the psychologist-treated group did not differ from the group who had continued to be treated by their GP on any of the subjective criteria measures at follow-up. The nature of the design precluded immediate post-treatment assessment, but even if this had been obtained the fact that it was not maintained over a relatively short period suggests a need for caution in claims for the benefits for patients of therapeutic intervention in primary health care.

Leaving aside the question of whether those patients seen by psychologists do benefit from this contact the problem highlighted by McPherson and Feldman (1977) still remains: there are far more patients seeking help from their GP for psychological problems than psychologists would be able to treat on a one-to-one basis. Any assessment of the advantages for patients of having psychologists working in primary health care should take into account all patients, not just those seen, but this issue has been largely ignored in reports of clinical psychologists working in this area. In addition, what of the patients who may not have access to a psychologist because of the latter's involvement in primary care? Clinical psychologists are a scarce resource, with less than 1,000 in Britain, expanding at only about 8 per cent each year (Kat, 1980a). Therefore, to the extent that the profession puts resources into primary health care, it is at best not increasing services or possibly even reducing them in other areas. In this way any benefits for patients at a primary care level may result in disadvantages for other groups of patients. Such decisions are likely to be opposed, if not by the patients themselves, by professionals in other fields who feel they are being deprived of services. Psychologists will have to be prepared to defend any decision to allocate resources in this direction when there are other areas, such as mental handicap, geriatrics and long-stay hospital patients, where in many parts of the country services are severely limited. At present they cannot draw on any clear support from studies on the effectiveness of interventions by psychologists and, while the practical advantages and convenience for the patient of being dealt with at a primary care level are generally accepted, they do not offer an overwhelming case. A final point that is rarely considered concerns the potential dangers of increased

availability of professional help for psychological problems. GPs have
been criticised for responding to psychological distress by prescribing
drugs because this carries the implication that the individual is suffering
from an 'illness' and may discourage him or her from attempting to
change any circumstances that are contributing to the distress. Clinical
psychologists whatever their orientation would aim to avoid this, but
having more psychologists functioning as therapists in group practices
and health centres might inadvertently strengthen the idea that
psychological distress needs specialised professional help, which carries
with it the risk that patients or existing primary care staff may become
reluctant to try to cope with such difficulties themselves.

Advantages for the NHS

Clinical psychologists have rapidly recognised that working within a
financially beleaguered National Health Service means that to receive
support any new development must be shown not just to be beneficial
to patients but also to lead to a more efficient use of existing resources
and preferably to a reduction in expenditure. As a result all of the
reports of psychologists working in primary health care attempt to
demonstrate that their interventions have not only been effective but
also cost-effective, using a variety of criteria. At a basic level it has been
argued that the number of contact sessions with a psychologist for
effective involvement is fairly low (e.g. McAllister and Philip, 1975;
Ives, 1979; Koch, 1979; Clark, 1979). Another obvious issue is what
would happen to those patients seen by psychologists if such a service
were not available. There is general agreement that a substantial
proportion of those who are treated by psychologists would normally
be dealt with by their GP. Therefore, it is important to consider
whether psychological intervention reduces the rate of GP consultation,
particularly as there is evidence that patients with psychological
problems have higher rates of consultation than other groups of
patients (e.g. Hassall and Stillwell, 1977). Related to this is the most
common form of treatment by the GP, prescribing psychotropic
medication, which has become a major issue due to the increase in the
extent of prescribing, the cost of this to the NHS and concern about
the long-term effects of certain of the most widely prescribed drugs,
particularly the benzodiazepines previously thought to be 'safe'. In
1961 32 million such prescriptions were issued in the United Kingdom,
costing about £7 million, while by 1973 the figure had risen to 45
million prescriptions at a cost of £22 million (Marks, 1978). The
evidence concerning the possible harmful effects of the benzodiazepines

is less clear; Marks, in reviewing the area, concluded that the dependence risk factor for the benzodiazepines is low, but more recently reports in the media (e.g. Doyle, 1980) have suggested that the widespread use of these drugs has negative consequences both at an individual and a social level and have recommended that increased clinical psychology and similar services in primary care could be a more desirable alternative.

Ives (1979) and Koch (1979) examined both consultation rates and psychotropic prescribing for patients treated by psychologists, and found evidence of significant reductions in both areas, which were maintained at follow-up. As with with possible advantages for patients, however, a rather different picture emerges in this area when Earll and Kincey's (1980) controlled evaluation is considered. They employed a series of objective outcome criteria including the pattern and frequency of prescriptions given and the frequency of GP consultations. On examining the use of these resources between the date of actual or potential referral and date of follow-up seven months later no significant differences were found between the group treated by the psychologist and the control group treated by their GP. When the use of resources was restricted to the period from referral to discharge for the psychologist-treated group and an estimated equivalent for the control group it was found that the former had received significantly fewer prescriptions for psychotropic medication suggesting that psychological intervention may produce a short-term reduction in prescribing rates but that there is a problem in ensuring maintenance of this effect. During the intervention period the two groups did not differ on consultations with the GP. Earll and Kincey (1980) interpret their findings as indicating that psychologists working in this area must look very closely at the optimal ways of using limited time and manpower.

The general issue of cost-effectiveness of intervention with psychological problems is exceedingly complex (see e.g. Chapman, 1979) and it would be unreasonable to criticise the above studies for failing to cover all aspects of this; rather they deserve recognition for attempting to tackle it at all. It is important, however, to realise that even if one can demonstrate that the involvement of psychologists has influenced cost-benefit variables, this is not the same as demonstrating that a clinical psychology service is cost-effective. For example if the prescribing of psychotropic drugs were consistently reduced for those patients who receive psychological treatment, this would not necessarily mean that an increase in clinical psychologists functioning as individual therapists at primary care level would lead to a significant reduction in the cost to the NHS for such medication, given the estimate that 8 per cent of the population of the United Kingdom are receiving psychotropic drugs (Marks, 1978). Similarly the likelihood of an overall impact on GP consultation rates would seem minimal. If clinical psychologists are serious in wishing to operate efficiently as well as effectively it is essential that they are prepared to regard cost-benefit analysis not just as a convenient support for developments they wish to make anyway, but as a real basis for decision-making about the allocation of resources and the nature of the services to be provided.

Advantages for GPs

As the group who are currently bearing the load of psychological problems in primary health care it might be expected that GPs would perceive definite advantages in greater involvement by clinical psychologists at this level. Support for this comes from two reports by Davidson (1977, 1979) involving questionnaire surveys of GPs concerning the kinds of working relationships they would like to have with psychologists. GPs had to indicate which of a variety of assessment, treatment and teaching facilities they would be interested in, together with the type of access to such a service and where it should be based. Both surveys indicated that there was a demand for psychological services, particularly in the areas of intellectual assessment and the treatment of sexual/marital, phobic, obsessional and habit disorders, but it is of interest that having psychologists working from the health centre or surgery was the least popular option with GPs, as this contrasts sharply with psychologists' own enthusiasm for becoming members of the primary care team. Davidson has suggested that the GPs response may simply be due to lack of facilities to accommodate extra personnel. However, an alternative interpretation could be that while GPs are interested in being able to refer patients to psychologists, they do not recognise them as having a particular role in primary health care. The published views of GPs who have had experience of working with psychologists have been generally favourable though not without reservations (e.g. Pritchard, 1978; Taylor, 1978). A number of joint publications by psychologists and GPs have indicated a gradual shift, from regarding psychologists mainly in a therapeutic role to recognising that they possess certain skills which they may be able to pass on to the GP and other members of the primary care team (e.g. Bhagat *et al.*, 1979; Coupar and Kennedy, 1980). Predominant among these skills are those involved in behaviour therapy (e.g. France, 1979; Hambly and Paxton, 1979), but as yet there is an absence of information concerning the extent of GPs interest in learning and applying such therapeutic skills.

In general it would appear that there would be advantages for GPs in establishing closer links with clinical psychologists but so far these appear to have been limited to a source of referral for certain patients, with the possibility of a subsequent reduction in consultation rates for these individuals, and to attempting to introduce some of the psychologists' skills into their own practice. The question arises, however, as to whether this is what would be most beneficial, or simply what psychologists are choosing to make available. One of the few studies which has set out without the presupposition that the psychologist knows what the GP needed was carried out by Broome (1978). This involved a survey of patients whom GPs identified as presenting management difficulties, together with an examination of the resources available to the GP. The findings that emerged concerning the complexity of the patients' and GPs' needs and the range of existing, if not fully utilised, facilities, suggest that the assumption that making available more specialist services is the most effective way to help the GP is open to question. Hopefully this might encourage other psychologists to engage in some basic assessment of the market's needs before offering their wares!

At present the whole area of how GPs regard psychological problems and the potential contribution of specialist services is rather confused. Cooper (1964), in a study of GPs attitudes to psychiatry, found that a majority regarded psychological problems as more difficult to deal with than other types of case, and most considered themselves inadequately trained and equipped for the treatment of such patients. Winter and Whitfield (1980), however, found that the vast majority of GPs in their sample agreed that the treatment of emotional problems is a major part of a GPs' work and felt competent in this field. This difference in findings could be seen as reflecting improvements in training in the period between the two studies being carried out. This contrasts, however, with the findings of a more general survey into primary health care by Cartwright and Anderson (1979) which suggested that there had been an actual decline between 1964 and 1977 in the proportion of GPs who thought that it was appropriate to be consulted about family problems, and that younger doctors regarded this as less appropriate than older ones. Future studies of GPs' attitudes to increased involvement by psychologists in primary health care will need to place this in the broader context of GPs' perception of psychological problems, of their own role in managing these and of all services available to them. A preliminary investigation by Eastman and McPherson (1980) suggests that in these circumstances the GP's view of psychologists' contribution is considerably more limited than that of psychologists themselves.

Advantages for Clinical Psychologists

It is perhaps not surprising that there are few references in the literature to what clinical psychologists themselves might gain by moving into primary health care. One would not after all expect members of the legal profession to argue for legislation to cover a new area on the grounds that it would bring them more work. However there is an important difference in that for the lawyer more work brings greater material rewards, which is not the case for psychologists. At present there are only a few clinical psychologists funded to work exclusively in primary health care, and there seems little likelihood of any growth in these numbers given current financial restrictions and priorities of the NHS. Even if such restraints did not apply there would be no financial incentive to move into this area. Neither do career prospects in terms of promotion seem of vital importance, as if they were clinical psychologists would have moved in greater numbers into fields such as mental handicap where there have been vacant established posts at all levels for many years (Mulhall, 1980). Similarly the shortage of manpower in mental handicap suggests that identified need is not a major factor in determining psychologists' interest in working in a particular area. It would seem likely that clinical psychologists are not motivated either by basic material rewards nor by altruism, but rather by job satisfaction in terms of operating an effective service within an interesting working environment.

It has been argued that operating within the psychiatric system is often not only inappropriate, in that this deals with a very small proportion of people with psychological problems, but also that this may be counterproductive to the clinical psychologist's approach as patients tend not to be referred on to the psychologist until their problems are well-established, by which time they have frequently adopted a passive role with regard to treatment which has to be overcome before effective intervention can be achieved. In addition psychologists' relationships with their psychiatric colleagues have sometimes been characterised by mutual suspicion and misunderstanding, leading to psychologists having to operate a more restricted service than they would wish because the ultimate authority within the system remains with psychiatrists. Therefore, primary health care has been seen as offering both the opportunity to operate more effectively and to establish independence, because although GPs may retain overall responsibility for their patients they are thought less likely to perceive clinical psychologists as challenging their area of expertise, and as such unlikely to attempt to impose restrictions on psychologists' work. One factor that has been ignored in this context is that at present psychologists have only had contact with a limited number of GPs and typically those who are keen to develop these links. As such it may be misleading to generalise from these experiences to working with GPs as a whole.

As these advantages for psychologists are rarely directly referred to in the reports of those working in the area it is not possible to assess whether or not they have been achieved, though the continuing expressions of enthusiasm and desire for expansion, together with frequent references in job advertisements to opportunities for working in primary health care, suggest that psychologists are finding satisfaction in working in this setting. As acknowledged above it would be unreasonable to adopt the puritanical position that because psychologists are enjoying what they are doing they cannot be doing any good. Clinical psychologists, however, should be careful to avoid copying the better established professions and confusing improvements for the profession with improvements in the service it provides.

Possible Roles for the Psychologist in Primary Health Care

The above review is not intended to suggest that clinical psychologists do not have a worthwhile contribution to make in primary health care, rather to question the direction which is currently being taken. The emphasis on the therapeutic role seems unlikely to lead to marked advantages for the majority of patients, for the NHS, for GPs and other members of the primary health care team, nor even in the long run for clinical psychologists themselves. In view of this it is rather surprising that some of the early publications in this area (e.g. Broadhurst, 1972; Kincey, 1974) indicated greater awareness of the possibility of a variety of roles for psychologists than some of the more recent ones (Ives, 1979; Koch, 1979), though there have been a growing number of calls for a more detailed consideration of how psychologists might operate in this setting (e.g. Kat, 1978; Hood, 1979; McPherson, 1980). This suggests that the profession is not entirely unaware of the limitations of therapeutic involvement but that it may be finding it difficult to establish new roles. When placed in a situation of uncertainty such as this, it seems that clinical psychologists (as a behaviourist might predict) simply emit behaviour at strength, which for the profession is treating people. Therefore the reluctance to try out new roles in primary health care may not be due to a lack of awareness of the problems inherent in the existing one, rather due to confusion as to what else might be done and how to bring about changes in practice. Some possible roles for psychologists working in primary health care are outlined below together with the implications for developing them.

Therapist

Having criticised clinical psychologists for focusing almost exclusively on the therapeutic role it may seem rather perverse immediately to return to it. However, it has not been argued that psychologists should abandon therapy, which is after all currently the profession's major area of skills, rather that it should be used more carefully, with a view to achieving specific goals as against regarding it simply as a means of dealing with psychological problems arising in primary health care. It could be argued that therapeutic skills are clinical psychologists' major attraction for GPs and hence that they offer a 'ticket of entry' into the area. However, an important lesson may be learned from the many patients with psychological problems who use a minor physical ailment as a 'ticket of entry' to see the GP, and who never get the opportunity to discuss what really concerns them because the GP is, or chooses to be, unaware of the underlying implications. Similarly, using therapy to establish credibility can act as a double-edged sword, as, while it is certainly unlikely that GPs will be interested in someone who has not demonstrated that he has a specific contribution to make, achieving credibility as a therapist may not establish credibility for any other role. Indeed it may lead to the psychologist being trapped in that role by a deluge of referrals and the creation of expectations. Therefore, if therapy is used as a means of establishing contacts and credibility, it is advisable to make it clear from the outset that this is only one of a number of possible contributions that clinical psychologists might be able to make.

If therapy is being offered the question arises whether to operate an unselective or a selective policy with regard to referrals, i.e., whether to accept any patient who might potentially be helped by psychological intervention, or whether to offer to treat only certain types of patient or problems. The former, which results in a heterogeneous sample of patients, has been the approach most commonly operated by psychologists working in this area, but it has certain disadvantages. All hopes of being able to carry out early intervention can vanish under the impact of a series of referrals of patients who have long-established problems and who may well have been through the psychiatric system several times already. In fact such patients are often being cared for at the primary care level because it is thought that the psychiatric system has nothing further to offer them. There is an onus on the GP to provide continuing care for this group of patients and it may be tempting for clinical psychologists to take them into treatment to avoid accusations that they are only interested in patients with minor problems who are likely to undergo 'spontaneous remission' anyway. However the consequence of this is that the limited time that the psychologist has available is restricted to dealing with a very small number of patients for whom change is unlikely no matter how skilled the particular therapist. In such cases the psychologist may make a more useful contribution to the patient's management by operating in some of the ways considered below. Indeed the referral of patients for whom individual therapy would be inappropriate may provide useful opportunities for demonstrating alternative skills.

Simply excluding a small number of patients from therapy on the grounds of the intractability of their problem is still likely to leave a considerable number of possible referrals and the question of whether it is more desirable to operate as clinical psychology's equivalent of a GP or to operate to more selective policy. The concept of a general practitioner psychologist has some attractions, but given the scarcity of clinical psychologists and the limited time most are likely to have available to work in this area it is simply impractical. When it comes to identifying a particular group of patients with whom to work, however, there are no obvious guidelines for selection. The criteria of therapeutic effectiveness is not easily applicable, as it has been argued (e.g. Bandura, 1978) that the vast literature on therapeutic outcome is often of questionable relevance to real-life clinical intervention in traditional settings. Therefore it would seem even more suspect to use this as a basis for deciding with whom to work in primary health care where both the problems and the patients, while resembling those seen in traditional settings, may differ in important ways. Given this situation rather than simply continuing to work with those patients with whom psychologists have had most success in traditional settings and transferring the therapeutic practice developed there, it would seem desirable that an attempt be made to detail the types of problems most frequently presented in primary health care, and to develop skills which are specifically designed for this setting. This type of approach has been adopted by Shapiro *et al.* (1979), who in the context of a wider research programme on stress and coping in the occupational environment are currently evaluating the effect of brief eclectic psychotherapy with patients referred to GPs.

Even if it is demonstrated that there are therapeutic skills which are particularly valuable in primary care settings, is the clinical psychologist the most suitable person to apply them? There have been a number of reports of members of other professions carrying out therapeutic interventions in this area (e.g. Brook, 1967; Corser and Ryce, 1977; Graham and Sher, 1976; Temperley, 1978) and also a series of studies carried out by people with training in counselling rather than from traditional professional backgrounds (Meacher, 1976; Anderson and Hasler, 1979; Waydenfield and Waydenfield, 1979). The latter are particularly interesting because they appear to be dealing with a similar sample of patients as psychologists and achieving comparable results both as measured by subjective ratings of change and by objective criteria such as psychotropic prescribing and consultation rates (though like the majority of studies reviewed above these have not been controlled evaluations). More general support for the effectiveness of such workers comes from a recent review by Durlak (1979) comparing professional and para-professional helpers, in which he concludes that in terms of measurable outcome professional mental health education, training and experience do not appear to be necessary prerequisites for effective therapeutic intervention.

Included in the studies examined by Durlak are those involving staff who had a professional training though not in a mental health speciality, which raises the possibility of psychologists helping existing primary health care professionals to develop their skills in dealing with psychological problems. This is considered more fully below, but it is important to recognise that giving away skills raises an important issue. While it has frequently been argued that this is the only way that psychologists can hope to have any influence (e.g. Miller, 1969), others less publicly have pointed out that the established professions such as medicine and law have obtained power by the opposite strategy of ensuring that the practice of their skills is carefully restricted to members of the profession. It is also argued that simply giving away skills devalues them in the eyes of potential recipients. Therefore clinical psychologists may be faced with a conflict between the interests of the service and the interests of the profession. On the evidence available there would seem to be a good case for clinical psychologists helping to identify more effective and efficient forms of therapeutic intervention, but the case for the psychologist being the main therapeutic agent seems questionable. Therefore adopting a therapeutic role may be seen as serving the function of establishing contact and credibility with those currently working in primary health care and offering the chance to develop therapeutic strategies, but not as an end in itself.

Consultant

The model of the clinical psychologist working individually with the patient in primary health care appears to have transferred from traditional hospital-based work with patients experiencing so-called 'neurotic' disorders. There are, however, a number of important areas in which psychologists are involved where this is not the most prevalent approach, but where instead the psychologist operates through others, typically those already in direct contact with the patient. The psychologist is operating here as a trainer, adviser or more broadly as a consultant though this term may be avoided because of its existing usage in the NHS as a career grade for medical staff. This is a particularly common way of functioning when there are few psychologists available, such as in the fields of mental handicap and the elderly, and so may be an appropriate role for the clinical psychologist in primary health care. Caplan (1970) has distinguished between four levels of consultation and this model will be used to consider the possible contribution psychologists might make.

Client-centred Case Consultation.   In this the focus is on helping the consultee deal with an individual case, for example helping a GP deal with a particular patient. A number of clinical psychologists have referred to this developing informally as a result of their work in general practice settings (e.g. Griffiths, 1978; Bhagat *et al.*, 1979) and for the GP it certainly resembles a traditional way of using the medical consultant when referral is made for advice on management. In the case of referral to a medical consultant, however, the GP and the specialist share a similar basic training and a model within which to interpret the problem, which makes it quite a different situation from referral to a psychologist. These problems of conflicting assumptions and language systems between family practitioners and behavioural scientists in the USA have been highlighted by Wales (1978). Therefore while advising on individual cases may prove a useful role for the psychologist, it is likely to be more effective where the psychologist has previously operated as a consultant at the next level.

Brook (1978) describes a somewhat different approach to this type of consultation in primary care in that it derives from a psychodynamic orientation and focuses on providing support for the GP or other team member in coping with the problems and anxieties they themselves experience in dealing with particular patients. While this approach may not appeal to psychologists who do not share this orientation, the nature of the interpersonal aspects of working relationships between consultant and consultee stressed by Brook and his colleagues remain an important consideration for those wishing to operate in this way.

Consultee-centred Case Consultation.   This is aimed at helping the consultee develop skills that will be useful in a range of future cases rather than just in dealing with a particular individual. It has been suggested that this could be a potentially important role for the clinical psychologist in primary health care (e.g. McPherson and Feldman, 1977) given that the vast majority of psychological problems are being dealt with by GPs, health visitors and other team members who may have had insufficient practical training for this aspect of their work. The difficulty that arises is in identifying what are the most appropriate skills in which to offer training. The skills which psychologists themselves have so far implied may be most useful are those involved in behavioural therapy and as mentioned above it has been argued that this could be employed much more widely by GPs (e.g. Hambly and Paxton, 1979). Behaviour therapy, however, has been used by psychologists in conditions very different from those of the average GP consultation with a patient which is estimated to last about six minutes. Ives (1979), for example, reports reducing the length of sessions from 45 to 30 minutes due to 'pressure of referrals' while working in general practice. It is possible that some GPs who are particularly interested in the behavioural approach to psychological problems might be prepared to set aside time to work in this way, but the likelihood of their being able to deal with more than a small proportion of patients seeking help seems remote given existing demands on their services, and the attraction of this to GPs as a whole seems likely to be minimal. France (1979) and Hambly and Paxton (1979) have suggested that it is possible for a GP to use the behavioural approach in normal consultations and support for this comes from Tapp *et al.* (1978) and Brockway (1978), based on work in the USA. If low involvement strategies along these lines could be developed and demonstrated to be effective this would seem a more practical contribution than traditional therapy.

A possible objection to this view could be that it implies a simplistic, 'techniques' model of the behavioural approach which has been widely criticised (e.g. Yates, 1975; Feldman, 1976) in that it ignores both the importance of an understanding of the theoretical basis of the approach and much of what is involved in the therapeutic process. There are, however, certain aspects of the behavioural approach such as self-monitoring, target-setting and basic anxiety-management procedures, which may be of value when placed within the context of a behavioural rationale for the development and maintenance of the problem. How this would compare to more detailed behavioural analysis and intervention or existing GP management is essentially an empirical question. The first step is for clinical psychologists to identify therapeutic strategies which the GP or other member of the primary health care team could use. This still leaves the problem of whether GPs generally would be interested in such procedures, particularly where additional training would be required. Davidson (1979) found that a high proportion of GPs in her survey expressed interest in having regular information about new psychological procedures, but there is a difference between being informed and actually getting involved. If it is hoped to change how GPs respond to the patient seeking help for psychological problems, then clinical psychologists may have to compromise between what they would like GPs to do and what GPs will be prepared to do. Therefore in some cases the goals may have to be limited to avoiding negative consequences, such as reinforcing an inappropriate illness model which encourages dependence and passivity in patients, rather than achieving positive ones such as the GP actively undertaking therapy.

Programme-centred Administrative Consultation.   This involves assisting the consultee in setting up, running and evaluating a particular programme. In Davidson's (1979) survey 57 per cent of GPs expressed an interest in research, and the wide variety of issues into which practising GPs carry out research is shown by the range of papers in the *Journal of the Royal College of General Practitioners* and similar publications. Many of these involve setting up programmes to deal with commonly occurring problems arising in primary health care, and although there has been an increasing emphasis on GPs receiving training in research skills (e.g. Howie, 1979), the extensive training of clinical psychologists in designing and evaluating programmes would suggest that this is an area where they could make a useful contribution. As yet, however, there have been no reports of psychologists working

solely as programme consultants in primary health care. The closest
they have come to this is running joint programmes, where they are
participants as well as advisers. Coupar and Kennedy (1980) describe
such a situation in the evaluation of a weight-control group run jointly
by a clinical psychologist and a GP. Working together in this way has
the advantage of allowing the psychologist to act as a consultant with
regard to the skills involved in the intervention as well as in organising
the programme. However, while existing areas of knowledge and skills
may make a good starting point, if psychologists are going to maximise
this form of contribution it would seem important for them to
develop the role to cover programmes which do not involve psychological treatment. Similarly GPs are not the only members of the
primary health care team who might benefit from such advice, indeed
health visitors, practice nurses and other staff may have more to gain,
given the relatively small amount of training they receive in programme
design and evaluation.

Consultee-centred Administrative Consultation.   In this the focus is
on helping the consultee to function more effectively, with a particular
emphasis on communication and organisational skills. One of the
earliest areas of collaboration between psychologists and GPs was in
doctor-patient communication (Ley and Spellman, 1967), and more
recently this has been identified as an area in which psychologists can
contribute to GP training. Pendelton *et al.* (1978) and Pendelton and
Tate (1980) have described a communication skills research programme
currently being carried out in the Oxford region. This consists of an
analysis of patients' reactions to their contact with GPs and communication difficulties identified by GPs, combined with training in verbal and
non-verbal communication skills. This is an attempt not just to improve
mutual satisfaction with consultations between GPs and patients, but
to tackle the key question of patients' compliance with instructions and
advice, which has been found generally to be low and related to the
doctor-patient relationship (Peck, 1978). The research by Pendelton and
his colleagues has capitalised on the fact that doctors wishing to
specialise in general practice are now having to take part in regionally
organised training schemes. These schemes provide a practical structure
within which the psychologist might function in a consultative role,
and as in the above study combine this with research.

     There is, however, an earlier stage at which future GPs already are
in contact with psychologists, that is, during the psychology or
behavioural science courses now undertaken by the majority of medical

students following the recommendations of the Todd Report (1968) on medical education. The content of such courses and the methods of teaching and assessment that have been employed have been the source of considerable debate with regard to their relevance to actual clinical practice (e.g. Griffiths, 1976; Channon and Walker, 1977). This problem has been tackled directly in a programme described by Weinmann (1978), in which medical students in their second pre-clinical year are given structured experience of interviewing patients in a general practice setting with feedback from their tutors and fellow students. There is particular emphasis on the patients' perception and interpretation of the symptoms and placing these in their psychosocial context. While there is no evidence as yet concerning the long-term effects of such training it would seem that, if nothing else, it would make the recipients more open later in their careers to seeing the relevance of a psychologist's contribution to their work, than would a watered-down version of an undergraduate psychology course.

Improving the organisational skills of those working in primary health care has become of increasing importance with the growth of group practices and health centres in which a variety of professions work together (Reedy, 1979) and this has been recognised as a relevant aspect of GP training (Irvine, 1979). This would appear an area in which psychologists could make a contribution, and so it is encouraging that the British Psychological Society submitted evidence to the DHSS Working Group on the Primary Care Team (BPS, 1979) pointing out the existence of relevant psychological literature on the structure and operation of groups and networks, and suggesting that area psychology services may be able to help primary health care teams to improve their functioning and to overcome difficulties that may arise. It should be noted, however, that the British Psychological Society offered to submit evidence, rather than being invited to do so, suggesting that psychologists are not immediately thought of when this feature of primary health care work is being considered. This is perhaps not surprising, given that the majority of those psychologists who are operating within primary health care are not necessarily specialists in the aspects of organisational and social psychology relevant to these problems, nor would they necessarily see this as part of their role. If psychologists are going to function as consultants at this level then they will need to consider what skills they will require and what knowledge base they are going to draw on, together with the implications for training.

Researcher. In addition to acting as research advisers to those already working in primary health care, this area offers considerable scope for psychologists to carry out their own research. One of the factors which distinguishes clinical psychologists from the majority of NHS staff is their extensive training in research methodology both at an undergraduate and postgraduate level. Therefore the low priority given to research by clinical psychologists interested in working in primary health care in Broadhurst's (1977) survey may seem rather surprising. This is reflected, however, in the absence of published research from this group with the exception of studies examining the contribution of the psychologist as therapist. It appears either that these psychologists have failed to appreciate the potential for research now open to them or, if they are aware of it, to see this as a relevant role. Examples of the issues that could be examined come from work carried out by psychologists outside the NHS and by workers with other professional backgrounds. A series of studies undertaken by researchers at the MRC Unit for Epidemiological Studies in Psychiatry, Edinburgh, have examined factors influencing patients' decisions to seek help from their GP and demonstrated the complexity of the interaction between physical, social and psychological variables (e.g. Ingham and Miller, 1979). Medical sociologists have also paid considerable attention to aspects of primary health care, notably how it is perceived both by patients and GPs (e.g. Cartwright and Anderson, 1979), its role in health education (e.g. Spencer, 1979) and the social meaning of prescribing practices for psychological problems (e.g. Cooperstock and Lennard, 1979).

Few psychologists who are interested in working in primary health care would deny that these are relevant areas of research. Why then have they shown limited interest in carrying out this research themselves? One reason may be the tendency to draw a distinction between providing a service and undertaking research. Many clinical psychologists, although listing research as an aspect of their work, would regard their role as predominantly that of service provider, seeing research as an extra to be fitted in when convenient if at all. This may be related to the research training they have experienced where often the questions addressed are chosen because they fit the requirements of a tidy experimental design rather than because of their practical implications. In addition although psychologists may talk about working in primary health care they are normally actually working in one or two group practices, and the demands of working in these practices may not coincide with the type of work which would result in a more general contribution to primary health care within a particular district or region, let alone on a national level. It has been argued above that, even if providing a therapeutic service in primary health care could be shown to be effective, it could not be an efficient use of scarce psychologist resources. On the other hand research examining why people seek help, how they respond to the help that is offered and how the current service might be made to function more effectively could result in psychologists having a more widespread influence. Suggestions along these lines in relation to the preventative side of primary health care have been made by Kat (1980b) but it will require a major shift in how clinical psychologists perceive research and its relation to service provision if such issues are going to be tackled by them as part of their contribution to primary health care.

Conclusions

The major weaknesses underlying clinical psychologists' move into primary health care is that it has taken place in a theoretical, organisational and resources vacuum. On a theoretical level, with the exception of some loosely formulated ideas about early intervention and community care, there has been no real attempt to develop new models of practice. The result has been that models, and particularly the therapeutic ones, which are currently predominant in hospital-based services have simply been transferred from their existing settings without questioning their relevance to primary care. If clinical psychologists are going to go beyond the important but ultimately limited role of being therapists then it will be necessary to broaden the theoretical and knowledge base of the profession to incorporate considerably more than most training courses currently on offer from those areas of psychology and related disciplines such as medical sociology which are relevant to understanding the social and organisational functioning of a primary health care service. Once this is established it may be possible to identify more clearly the skills that clinical psychologists will require to make a worthwhile contribution in this field. At an organisational level, there is a need to consider how working in primary health care fits in with overall planning of clinical psychology services. At present developments seem more often to reflect personal interests rather than co-ordinated plans. The Trethowan Report's (1977) comments on clinical psychology's contribution to primary care are frequently quoted as if placing this development in a more general structure for services, but Trethowan has tended to become the bible for the profession in more ways than one, as it too is being quoted out of context, with those bits which do not suit the argument being missed out. Clinical psychologists at a local and possibly even a national level will have to decide on the emphasis to be placed on this development in services in relation to others, and to do this requires identifying more clearly not just what psychologists want to do in primary health care but what they might most usefully do.

The question of resources is probably the most immediately important one, as without sufficient resources no new service is likely to develop on a worthwhile scale. Therefore the present financial restrictions on the NHS together with criticisms by government ministers of excessive usage of primary health care facilities by people who expect 'a pill for every ill' (Jenkin, 1980), do not bode well for a major growth in psychologists working in this area. Paradoxically, however, this may actually be beneficial, if it forces clinical psychologists to consider much more carefully what developments are likely to have most impact. Discussions are currently taking place about the formation of a joint standing committee between the British Psychological Society and the Royal College of General Practitioners to deal with matters of mutual interest and concern. Therefore this would seem a highly appropriate time for clinical psychologists to reconsider the possible contribution that might be made to primary health care. In doing so it would be useful to examine the much larger scale move by American psychologists from hospital to community-based services (see e.g. Heller and Monahan, 1977). This development took place in the 1960s in the context of a major reorganisation of mental health services, with large-scale financial support by federal government, circumstances which in comparison to those now facing psychologists in Britain may seem ideal. Nevertheless, reviews of what has been achieved by this move into the community, not only by psychologists but by the whole range of mental health professions, suggest that there is no clear evidence of advantages for patients or of widespread changes in the nature of service provision from that found in traditional settings (e.g. Chu and Trotter, 1974; Windle *et al.*, 1974). This situation has been described as 'innovation without change' (Rappaport, 1977) — a phrase that clinical psychologists should bear in mind when considering their move into primary health care, as it is to be hoped that this is one aspect of American psychology that need not be replicated here.

3 THE EDUCATIONAL PSYCHOLOGIST AS INSTIGATOR AND AGENT OF CHANGE IN SCHOOLS: SOME GUIDELINES FOR SUCCESSFUL PRACTICE

Robert Burden

The recent publication of the results of the investigation by Michael Rutter and his colleagues into the effects of within-school variables on the attendance, attainments and behaviour of pupils attending twelve London secondary schools (Rutter *et al.*, 1979) has helped to highlight a growing trend amongst educational psychologists in England and Wales. By placing its primary emphasis upon the ways in which schools can influence their pupils, the Rutter Report, as it has come to be known, has helped to draw the attention of the teaching profession in particular to the fact that problems do not always, or even usually, arise from within individual pupils. Children who do not learn, or are disruptive or otherwise disturbing, need not necessarily be unintelligent, maladjusted or otherwise disturbed. They may in fact be responding to an educational system that leaves them with little option but to act in just those ways.

Thus the trend amongst some educational psychologists (by no means the majority to date) has been to seek ways in which they can gain greater understanding of how institutions like schools have an affect on those who are forced to attend them. There are at least two major premises that underlie such an approach. The first is that the problems of individuals can only be understood within the context of the systems within which they live and work. The second is that it is more likely to be the system that is in need of change than the individual. The latter premiss will not always be true, but even when it isn't, it is highly unlikely that any individual will be able to change without corresponding change within the system.

Thus it can be argued that educational psychologists need to become effective systems analysts and systems engineers if they are to play any really valuable role within schools. Such a viewpoint stands in marked contrast to the more traditional view of the educational psychologist's role, which took the individual child as its focus and attempted by means of psychometric and/or clinical techniques to discover within-child variables to account for learning failure, behaviour difficulties, etc. The inadequacies of such an approach were due not only to the inefficiency and lack of validity of many of the most commonly used techniques, but also because it often failed to take into account the interactive nature of problems and the context within which they occurred. Even more importantly, it provided little opportunity for the psychologist to affect the situation in which learning failure or disturbing behaviour was taking place since the problem was accepted as emanating from the child. Dissatisfaction amongst many educational psychologists with such a model led to a great deal of discussion about their professional role, both within the pages of the *Journal of the Association of Educational Psychologists* during the late 1970s and in an important book of essays, *Reconstructing Educational Psychology* (Gillham, 1978). The systems approach to which this chapter refers itself is only one of a number of positive attempts to get to grips with the very real problems that the more traditional approach chose to ignore.

Unfortunately, the Rutter Report is of limited value to us here, mainly because it advocates a nomothetic approach to what is in many ways an ideographic problem. What I mean by this is that Rutter and his colleagues have taken a traditionally psychometric correlational approach to the gathering of data within schools in the apparent hope that something meaningful will arise out of their statistical analyses that will be applicable to all secondary schools. Thus they would argue that by accumulating ever more data from a larger sample of schools they would be more likely to measure reliably the process of schooling. Our need on the other hand is to understand the unique way in which individual schools have a specific effect upon those (pupils and teachers) who interact within them. A *post hoc* correlational approach will never enable us to do this, though it may throw up one or two good ideas on the way.

I have argued elsewhere (Burden, 1978; 1981) that an understanding and application of systems theory can provide the practising educational psychologist with a good basis from which to begin working within schools, particularly if the latter are large and complex as is the case with most comprehensive schools. I shall therefore devote this paper to some practical suggestions of important keystones to success with the systems approach. I shall suggest that within any systems project there are four crucial stages during each of which the work of the systems team or its various members will differ along certain predictable dimensions. The purpose of the following section will be to describe each of these stages in turn, together with the requirements to be met in order to achieve successful outcomes.

Stage One: Preparation

This is the most crucial stage of all in many respects, but also the one that is most likely to be overlooked or carried out inadequately. The key phrase here is taken from a seminal paper by Georgiades and Phillimore (1975), and is referred to as 'cultivating the host culture'. Basically, what is meant here is that too much time cannot possibly be spent in preparing the ground and setting up a school-based project that is likely to succeed.

Within this stage there are certain essential prerequisites. The most likely attributes for success are respect, trust and liking. The more people who see the change agent(s) in these terms the more likely it is that his suggestions will be followed. Some educational psychologists place too much emphasis on the 'liking' attribute, and see warm relationships with their schools as being of vital importance. This can be overemphasised. Warm relationships in themselves will not bring about change; in fact too warm a relationship can sometimes lead to collusion in bad practice. Slightly less warmth, and a good deal more professional respect, is likely to produce more effective results in the long run. In action terms this means that no time spent in a school can possibly be wasted, particularly if this means having coffee or lunch with different members of staff listening to their problems, straightening out their misapprehensions and shaping up their expectations. The purpose here is:

to 'get a feel' of the school and its approach to education;
to find out who are the high formal and informal status members of
    the staffroom, and to establish these as allies;
to work out where the power structure lies;
to gain a grasp of staff satisfactions and dissatisfactions;
to sort out where the school's educational priorities lie;
to obtain some idea of the 'tone' of the school, both from its
    appearance and from observations of teacher–teacher,
    teacher–pupil and pupil–pupil interactions.

All of this is concerned with building up a realistic picture of the need for and openness to change. A basic rule also cited by Georgiades and Phillimore (1975) is that one should always start with a potential winner, even though such an institution might seem far less in need of radical change than many other schools on one's patch.

Possibly the most crucial variable here is likely to be the nature of the headteacher, without whose implicit and explicit support no project will work. It is thus absolutley essential to start one's first project of this kind in a school where the headteacher not only understands and agrees with the way in which you want to work, but also has the backing and support of his staff in general on matters of educational concern. The headteacher is the person with whom you must necessarily be primarily identified if any change is to be brought about, since his is invariably the most profound within-school influence. It can sometimes happen that an unpopular or weak headteacher can have all his change efforts sabotaged by an unsympathetic staff, but within our educational system the power tends to lie with the head and his is the backing you will most need. There is one further point of considerable importance in one's dealings with headteachers when 'change projects' are being considered. This is that the project is far more likely to be successful if the original suggestion comes from the head himself. There are various ways in which this can be primed to happen, but the general rule is that if a headteacher asks for psychological intervention of a wider nature than the traditional referral model then he and his school are far more likely to be committed to its success.

Even at this point there is still a great deal of preparation to be carried out. The proposed project is almost certain to be associated with a particular problem or set of problems as perceived by the head and his staff (although I do know of some instances where an educational psychologist has been asked by the head to carry out a general systems analysis on his school). This is likely to have taken the form of something like 'Do you think it might be possible to look at our provision for remedial pupils with the school?' or, 'I wonder if you could help us to find ways of looking at the behaviour problems that we seem to be having with our fourth year non-examination pupils?' The next task, therefore, will be to seek some form of clarification of the problem, by asking through a series of informal discussions with individual staff members and more formal meetings with senior management or departmental staff, such questions as,

'How did the problem first come to be noticed?'
'Do different members of staff have different perceptions of what the problem is?'
'Is there anyone who doesn't concede that there's a problem at all?'
'Why is a solution important and to whom?'
'Is it possible that the problem with which you are presented is really the manifestation of a much deeper and more intractible problem?'

'Would you be likely to receive backing for deciding to tackle a different problem from the one with which you were originally presented?'

It is my experience, after several years' work in this kind of way, that remedial problems can never be considered solely within the context of the remedial department, and that behaviour problems will always involve the total organisation of the school and the relationship between curriculum and pastoral care.

It is at this point that the first major decision will need to be reached. Is there any point in going on or not? Systems theory argues that such a decision should be made as a result of some form of costs-benefits analysis. Are the benefits likely to accrue from your 'intervention' likely to outweigh the costs involved? Or, to put it in another way; given that resources (time, manpower, expertise, etc.) are limited, is there the prospect of a reasonable rate of return for systems effort employed – or might such effort be better employed elsewhere? If you can't predict with a reasonable degree of confidence some form of worthwhile benefits to the school and/or its pupils, there may well be no point in going on. If we assume, however, that an affirmative answer has been reached, we are now in a position to move on to stage two.

Stage Two: Planning and Implementing the Intervention

It is at this point that a project should begin to take a more cohesive form. The actual form itself will be dependent upon a number of factors even after careful preparation of the kind described above. Of course this will not be a strictly linear process, since some of the factors to be described now will undoubtedly have had some part to play in previous negotiations.

First, there is the need to establish your systems team. It is a universal rule of this kind of work that it cannot be successfully accomplished alone by the 'hero innovator' on his white charger. Even the Lone Ranger needed Tonto! There is a good deal of evidence, however, that a team consisting of two committed professionals can accomplish a great deal under certain conditions (Cocks and Gardner, 1979; Ainscow and Tweddle, 1977; Bailey and de Souza, 1980). In each of these examples there is evidence of educational change being accomplished by two-person teams in a way that far exceeds the expected sum of the contributions. The addition of a partner, mirror, soul-mate, call it what you will, can act both as a spur and a restraining influence, as well as someone with whom to share the toil. With the right partner, the psychological benefits can be immense. If in doubt in one's search for a partner, perhaps one's best source is the system to be studied itself. In a sense this team member (see 'consumer' below) will act as a 'mole' within the system, spreading the positive word wherever possible, looking for links with others of a like mind, feeling out the weak spots and danger areas. The kind of access to both formal and informal information about the system that such a team member has is invaluable since it is simply not available to the outsider, however close his contact or warm his relationship with the school.

There are at least six important roles to be performed by the systems team, none of which are mutually exclusive. Thus the same team member could theoretically function in several different roles, although I would argue that this is likely to impede the effective performance of that role to some extent. These roles are as follows.

(i)   The team leader should function as chairperson and spokesperson for the team. He/she should see it as his job to clarify what is going on and feed back information to both the team and the clients. It is absolutely essential that the person in this position exudes justifiable self-confidence and can maintain excellent morale within the team.

(ii) It is often the case that the team leader also feeds back written reports, but it is very useful, if the right kind of person is available, to have a *secretary* keeping continuous notes and arranging for up-to-date written reports on recent discussions and decisions to be made available.

(iii) Most of the spadework now will be in the hands of *systems engineers*, i.e. team members who have been allocated specific tasks such as assessing staff attitudes, interviewing pupils, investigating school record cards, evaluating diagnostic testing procedures in use, etc. A large team can afford two members on each of such tasks, and will benefit from this as a comparison of perceptions is always useful. Within a small team one person may well have to carry out several tasks. The secret is in working out carefully beforehand the kind of information that is most likely to be useful.

(iv) It is always worthwhile having a strong *statistician/psychometrician* in the team, if one is available. This should help to ensure that any conclusions or inferences you draw are likely to be based on facts.

(v) Similarly, *an expert in one or another of the areas under investigation* will be valuable, e.g. a psychologists' team might well include a remedial advisory teacher, specialist adviser and/or social worker.

(vi) One of the most important people on the team will be a *consumer* i.e. someone working within the system with at least high informal status. If he/she has high status at both a formal and informal level, so much the better.

Once a systems team has been gathered it is essential that the team leader establishes the concept of team-work, and continues to ensure that the product of any work carried out is greater than merely the sum of a number of individual efforts. This cannot be emphasised too strongly and should be seen as the leader's most important role. As such it will involve a realistic appraisal of the team's strengths and weaknesses and should ensure that the project is properly scheduled and will have realistic goals. It is far better to set limited targets initially and to achieve these comfortably, than to aim too high and to suffer the frustration and depression that failure can bring. This latter point also helps to emphasise the importance of the secretarial role. It is often extremely difficult in this kind of work to stand back and observe realistically just what is being accomplished. Continuous feedback both to members within the team and to everyone involved in even the slightest extent will help to overcome inevitable periods of confusion, panic and depression. There is a very real sense in which this kind of work can be seen as action research, but as such it is 'messy' and confusing. Any sense of clarity and order that can be introduced in an ongoing way will undoubtedly strengthen the team and its sense of purpose.

The other most important aspect of this implementation stage is the establishment of a *contract*. Again this cannot be emphasised too highly. Again and again problems have arisen in projects of this kind as a result of misconceptions and misinterpretations as to what would be involved and what the participants have a right to expect. There is not space here to provide illustrations of contracts that we have actually established on our projects, but there are several important points that need to be considered. The contract will form the basis for the project team's work within the school and should provide the criteria by which the success of their intervention will eventually be judged. It should set realistic expectations for both sides, the intervenors and the recipients, and should be used at various times within the life of the project as a mirror for the progress that is being achieved. It is for this reason that I would advocate a fairly formal, almost ritualised set of procedures which would include a formal gathering of all those likely to be centrally involved in the project, especially the headteacher, a verbal set of agreements on certain key issues such as open access to personnel, files and homes, regular attendance at discussion meetings and continued feedback to the school on information gained and conclusions reached. In our projects we always have such a contract typed out and circulated for everyone to read, and then reconvene to give it a unilateral seal of approval or to make changes where necessary. It is extremely doubtful whether such a procedure is of any legal standing, but what it does do is to invest in the project a sense of commitment and importance that is often otherwise lacking. It also provides something 'concrete' that can be produced by either side in the event of difficulties in order to objectify and depersonalise disputes, should these arise.

Once the contract has been established and agreed upon, a valuable next move is to ensure that all the school staff are informed by a high-status member (headteacher or deputy) about the project and how it is likely to involve them personally. A brief description of the project by the team leader at a formal staff meeting is a helpful way of supplementing this, as also in a brief written summary to each member of staff individually.

Stage Three: Data Collection

Having defined the scope of your problem and prepared the ground for some form of intervention, you will now have set realistic goals within a reasonable time period, and have committed your team to gathering information of a kind that will enable decisions to be made about the need or otherwise for change. The very nature of the exercise means that you will be looking at the ways in which individuals are functioning and expected to function within a subsystem (classroom group, unit, department), or a larger system or organisation (school) which is in turn part of an ever widening set of systems (neighbourhood, community, town or city, country). You need first to decide how wide your analysis is going to be. Then you must decide what information you need about the functioning of different aspects of subsystems within the wider system.

Detailed information is available elsewhere of how to carry out a systems analysis (Beishon and Peters, 1972). However, there are a number of procedures that can be of great value to the educational psychologist involved in this kind of school-based project. Interesting ideas can be found in both Rutter *et al.* (1979) and Kelly (1979) but perhaps the best sourcebook here is that produced by Cohen (1976).

Stage Four: Pulling It All Together

By this point you will probably have accumulated a mass of data and a great deal of confusion. If the leader is doing his job properly, he will have ensured that throughout the regular discussions and feedback sessions a constant thread is maintained, using the original contract as a cornerstone. The team itself will need extra meetings to sort out where they're going and to exchange impressions of strong and weak links within the system. It is traditional to use flow-block diagrams as an aid in this sorting out process. This is not necessary, but can prove extremely helpful once the additional effort has been made to learn the conventions. After the data-gathering period has ended, the team should allow several sessions in which to put together a summary of their findings. At this point a written record of these findings should be made available to one or two key members of the 'consumers group'. A full and frank exchange of comments should take place at this juncture. It could well be that a 'mini' staff meeting may be called for here, during which the team members feed back orally to those members of staff most involved their conclusions drawn from the information gathered. Again, this is the place for any plain speaking that needs to be done.

Once agreement has been reached about any points at issue, the team leader or secretary should prepare a full and detailed report to be sent to the headteacher, with extra copies for distribution amongst other members of staff who are interested, e.g. copy for staffroom noticeboard. This report should include both conclusions drawn from the evidence gathered and the implications of these for the future organisation of the school. This need not involve specific recommendations for future action. A successful systems analysis need only make available clearly identified outcomes of any subsequent decisions about the organisation of the system. The object is to help administrators and others to make future decisions on a rational basis, not to offer solutions — that is the task of systems design.

General Conclusions

The suggestions made in this chapter were not arrived at overnight. Each of them has grown out of a series of single-school change projects in the Devon area stretching back over at least a six-year period. Some of these projects, particularly the most recent, have been remarkably successful not only in implementing change within comprehensive and special schools but also in receiving the approbation of teachers who have been willing to share with others their positive feelings about educational psychologists' working in this way. Other projects have been less successful, but *never* disastrous. Every project has been exciting, exhausting and worthwhile.

Lest it be thought that such work can only take place from a university base with a fairly large team and resources, I would argue that these are the very factors that have provided difficulties rather than removed them. Our projects have always been carried out from outside any LEA power base, and rarely with the backing of the kind of status carried by the local schools psychological service. A large team of trainees, moreover, can be quite a hindrance when they themselves are still acquiring the basic skills necessary for work of this kind. Every negative experience has provided a valuable lesson for future occasions. Much of what has been written here is a product of mistakes rather than of a series of smooth, error-free rides. It is, however, a mark of the potential power of this approach that we have never lacked a queue of schools requesting our intervention. Moreover, those who have left the Exeter training course prepared to work with at least *some* of their schools in this kind of way, rarely find it possible or desirable to revert to a more traditional model.

The final message, then, is clear. What is offered is an approach to the successful implementation of change in schools that can be brought about by the application of psychological skills within the framework of a systems team. The likelihood of such success is enhanced by a consideration of certain crucial factors and the development of appropriate strategies to overcome problems arising from such factors. The task is not an easy one, but it seems likely that the greatest mistake that educational psychologists have hitherto made has been a refusal to face up to just this fact.

4 EDUCATIONAL PSYCHOLOGISTS AND INNOVATION

R. P. Gregory

The intentions of this chapter are to set out some of the arguments for psychologists' need to innovate, examine some of the relevant literature on innovation, and list tentative hypotheses about factors which encourage or restrain an innovative psychologist.

Innovation has been defined by Dalin (1973) as 'a deliberate attempt to improve practice in relation to certain desired objectives'. There is some overlap with action research which Halsey (1972) described as 'small-scale intervention in the functioning of the real world and the close examination of the effects of such intervention'. Town (1973) saw affinities between action research, curriculum development, the social experiment, evaluation research (see Morris and Fitzgibbon, 1978, for a classification of evaluation research models) and programmes of systematic social action designed to promote change. Classical experimental design activity (Burroughs, 1970) could also be included.

> Action research can be described as a process whereby in a given problem area, research is undertaken to specify the dimensions of the problem in its particular context; on the basis of this evidence, a possible solution is formulated and is translated into action with a view to solving the problem; research is then used to evaluate the effectiveness of the action taken. (Town, 1973)

Such steps in the solution of a problem are made explicit in what has been called the 'systems approach' (Gagne and Briggs, 1974; Romiszowski, 1970; Stufflebeam, 1968; Stufflebeam *et al.*, 1971), or 'educational technology' (Hartley and Davies, 1978). The innovator has been called a 'change agent' (Georgiades and Phillimore, 1975), and this connects with organisational development (see Arends and Arends, 1977). It is important that the would-be innovator be aware of all these different but interrelated topics because all are useful, but rarely are the affinities pointed out in their distinct literatures.

The Need for Innovation

It will be the thesis here that innovation by educational psychologists is needed to help them define a scientifically based function. The urgent needs of the education system as a whole for innovative psychological practice have been argued by Sutton (1978a). Innovation and evaluation are not to be seen as appendages to an organisation to be used when time allows: jointly they provide an essential feedback loop for an organisation's activities. The Seebohm Report (1968) put the sentiment most strongly for social services, but it is equally applicable to education.

> The personal Social Services are large-scale experiments in helping those in need. It is both wasteful and irresponsible to set experiments in motion and omit to record and analyse what happens. It makes no sense in terms of administrative efficiency and however little intended, indicates a careless attitude to human welfare.

The Summerfield Report (Department of Education and Science, 1968) found that research played only a very small part of most psychologists' work, and that 'the lack of opportunities for research and reflection on the value of the work being undertaken, together with doubts about the quality and usefulness of some of it' were cited as particular reasons for leaving local authority work by those who had gone on to practice in other fields.

In support of the need for innovation in psychological practice in LEAs, let us examine the traditional and still widely practised work of educational psychologists (see, for example, Acklaw, 1979). They may be described as having three major functions:

(i)   administering admission to special schools;
(ii) clinical — treating individual children;
(iii) innovation.

Admission to Special Schools

Schools for the Educationally Subnormal (Mild).   The useful contribution of practising psychologists to this process would appear to be limited. The criteria for placement are so vague (Brindle, 1974) that it is possible for two psychologists working in the same building to disagree widely on a placement decision. Doubts about the effectiveness of ESN(M) schools in promoting pupils' attainments have been raised by Asher (1970), Presland (1970), Hodge and Bain (1971) and Ghodsian and Calnan (1977). Gardner (1977) has given an account of the various criticisms raised against category-based special education.

Before a child is placed in an ESN(M) school usual practice is that he is referred to a psychologist. Implicitly the school is probably asking questions like:

(i) is Johnny working 'to potential' or 'up to capacity'?
(ii) why is Johnny not making progress?

Examine question (i). Traditionally the psychologist has tried to provide an answer by using intelligence tests, commonly the *Wechsler Intelligence Scale for Children* or *Stanford-Binet*. Such action does not take account of the extensive literature denying that intelligence tests measure 'potential' (e.g. Crane, 1959; Gillham, 1974). In fact Vernon (1968) wrote

> . . . the worst sinners are the educational and child guidance psychologists who continue happily to interpret the Terman-Merrill or WISC IQ's . . . as measuring *potential* ability distinct from educational achievement and even to employ the motion of under-achievement which was current in the 1920s.

Some psychologists have attempted to answer the second question by resorting to the now discredited ability-training model, representing the 'internal-deviancy' (Gardner, 1977) approach to diagnostic-prescriptive teaching. 'Diagnostic tests' such as the *Illinois Test of Psycholinguistic Ability* and the *Frostig Developmental Test of Visual Perception* have been widely used. From their results it was hoped to identify children's strengths and weaknesses and to use this knowledge to design prescriptively-based programmes to remediate the presumed internal disabilities. Gardner (1977) wrote

> . . . the assumption is made that strengths in internal processes or abilities (e.g. perceptual, psycholinguistic) are necessary prerequisites to the effective learning of academic skills. Yet there is no suitable empirical support for the assumption that training or remediation of presumed perceptual or psycholinguistic weaknesses is a necessary prerequisite to academic skill attainment.

The task-analysis model represents a behavioural alternative to the internal-deviancy approach in diagnostic-prescriptive teaching. The child's behaviours are evaluated along various skill dimensions. No assumptions are made about internal abilities as in the ability-training model. This model, which has been extensively used for the last decade to design training programmes in the armed forces and industry (Budgett *et al.*, 1970; Hartley and Davies, 1978) has only recently begun to influence British education. Ainscow and Tweddle (1979) have described its use for children with reading problems. The best evaluative support comes from Becker (1977) who described how eight education programmes with differing theoretical bases were compared in an evaluation project involving 75,000 disadvantaged and/ or non-English-speaking American primary-age pupils. The most successful programmes used the direct instructional model (commercially available as DISTAR), and raised the attainments of pupils on average to American norms or above in three years. Such hierarchically task-analysed programmes of behavioural objectives render the traditional educational assessment by psychologists largely redundant.

Schools for the Maladjusted.   The 'psychological' criteria for admission to these special schools are even vaguer than those for the ESN(M) category. It is possible that the refusal of admission by ordinary school is a more important factor in the placement of some children in special school (Gregory, in press). Doubts about the effectiveness of maladjusted schools were raised by Roe (1965) and Vace (1972), and even the necessity for gross intervention in many cases by the finding of Pumfrey and Ward (1971) that 80 per cent of untreated maladjusted children 'showed a marked improvement in adjustment' when followed up four years later. Rutter and Madge (1976) quoted findings suggesting that primary schools themselves play a part in the generation of some problem children, and Rutter *et al.* (1979) confirmed this for secondary schools.

Psychologist as Clinician

Psychologists in child guidance centres have traditionally worked in a 'team' with social workers and psychiatrists. The effectiveness of such treatment has been questioned by Shepherd *et al.* (1966); Tizard (1973) and Levitt (1957). Many children get better without treatment. The finding of 80 per cent remission in an untreated group is similar to others (Levitt, 1957; McCaffrey and Cummings, 1969).

Medical and Behavioural Models.   This clinic-based treatment of
individual cases is based on a medical model of human behaviour. It has
resulted in clinical investigation centring on the child and intrapersonal
variables, and has rarely included an examination of the environmental
variables within the institution in which the child was functioning.
Reynolds and Murgatroyd (1977) said of research into school truancy:

> In part this neglect of the school situation of truanting children may
> reflect the inherent tendency of many psychologists turned educa-
> tional researchers whose education has trained them to individualise
> the explanation of personal problems in terms of personal pathology.

Rutter *et al.* (1979) have provided extensive evidence for the influence
of secondary schools on their pupils' behaviour, in line with Clarke's
(1978) contention that there has been a theoretical move away from
main-effect to interactionist or transactionist models of behaviour.
Gregory (in press) has cited some of the possible disadvantages of
psychologists' preoccupation with individual cases, the most serious
being the inadvertent collusion in covering up inadequacies in
education policy and the school system, and the active prevention of
schools from developing organisation-based problem-solving and
evaluative skills.

  With the advent of behaviour modification techniques a subtle
change of model is occurring. Increasingly psychologists are seeing that
the problems of some children are due to the teachers' management
techniques, or inadequacies in the teaching programme. Epidemiological
studies (e.g. Rutter *et al.*, 1970) have indicated that the prevalence of
children with educational problems is very high, and the Warnock
Report (1978) has suggested that future planning of services for
children should be based on the assumption that one in five at some
time during their school career would require some form of special
education provision. Albee (1968), Likorish and Sims (1971) and
Tyerman (1975) have emphasised that the delivery of service on an
individual, crisis-orientated basis to all members of the community
who need it would require huge increases in the numbers of professional
staff.

Recent Innovations.   Given that one of the aims of a psychological
service is to help children who are having problems and prevent others
developing them, the problem of service delivery is a real one. The
method of individual casework has grave disadvantages. As a

consequence some psychologists (Ainscow *et al.*, 1978; Harrop, 1974; Presland, 1978; Bevington *et al.*, 1978) are turning to in-service training of teachers and parents, as an alternative mode of helping children by teaching their primary caretakers new and demonstrably effective skills, and to consultation. If psychologists are not to make the same sort of mistakes as their predecessors they must ask two questions:

(i) what evidence is there for such a *modus operandi* having worked in the past — possibly drawing on sources outside of education;
(ii) has their own intervention worked, has it achieved its objectives, has the hypothesis been supported or refuted?

With respect to in-service training, the findings are at best equivocal. Georgiades and Phillimore (1975) have argued that the assumptions behind training as a strategy for inducing organisational change are based upon the psychological fallacy that since work oragnisations are made up of individuals we can change the organisation by changing its individual members: 'there is a plethora of evidence to refute this proposition'. They quoted educational research indicating that the effects of teacher training were nullified during the first year of teaching. From industry they described how despite first-class training the greatest influence upon a supervisor's behaviour in his plant was the leadership of his immediate boss.

> If the old way of doing things in the plant situation is still the shortest path to approval by the boss, then this is what the super-visor really learns. In order to effectively produce changes in behaviour some changes in his plant environment would also seem to be necessary. The training course alone cannot do it.

Katz and Kahn (1978) and Glen (1975) support this view.

In-service training for teachers in this country has not traditionally been characterised by evaluation, though there is now an increasing literature (Henderson, 1978). Course evaluation must focus firstly on efficient ways of having participants learn by the end of the course what the instructors set out to teach them. Watson (1972) found that course performance was greatly improved by contingent reinforcement. Secondly it must examine means by which the newly acquired skills can be maintained at the place of work. Neville (1978) described different strategies for in-service training, some involving on-the-job training. Thirdly it should address the question: has the course solved the problem that originally prompted its inception? Gagne and Briggs (1974), Budgett *et al.* (1970) and Hartley and Davies (1978) have indicated that the armed forces and industry have been very much concerned with the efficiency of instructional design.

Consultation as a style of working alternative to individual casework has been reviewed by Topping (1977). The results are at best equivocal.

In-service training and consultation carry implicit expectations of system-change, but some writers would like to see psychologists attempt explicit system-change intervention. Arends and Arends (1977) have suggested that, if just part of the energy that goes into one-to-one counselling and treatment for under-achievers and truants were made available, that would be more than enough to bring about important lasting change in systems and organisations. They saw the psychologist as a change agent. Medway (1975) has described the future role of the psychologist as a behavioural psychologist adept at reducing and containing the incidence of maladaptive social behaviours through consultation methods, organisational development, systems analysis and environmental restructuring. Some such intervention has been demonstrated by Burden (1978). Innovative psychologists, however, must circumscribe such endeavour with scientific evaluation.

Educational psychologists have failed to change significantly from their traditional role in the face of:

(a) accumulated evidence of the ineffectiveness of what they (and the institutions with which they are most closely connected) do;
(b) consumer dissatisfaction with the service.

The anticipation of the Summerfield Report had been that an increase in the numbers of practising educational psychologists would result in more attention being given to research and development, with a corresponding benefit for the education system in relation to problems of learning, teaching and school organisation. The lack of change is a phenomenon worthy of investigation in its own right.

Such an investigation must remember Clarke (1978)

... there is multiple determinism of behaviour *even that of psychologists* [present author's italics] and a continuous interaction both within the person and in the situation. A focus on the person alone or the environment alone is highly misleading.

As for personal variables, Quicke (1978) has suggested that

psychologists are limited in their reading of psychological literature, whilst Hargreaves (1978) has seen them as intellectually inferior to academic psychologists. These may be part reasons why research evidence has had such a limited impact upon educational psychologists.

Educational Psychologist as Innovator

Innovator Characteristics

These include:

1. exposure to innovative models;
2. experience of innovating;
3. intellectual skills and information;
4. position of innovator in hierarchy;
5. work-coping strategies.

It may be that after initial exposure to innovative models much is 'learned by doing', and that a project is successful because the innovator has worked with innovative people and already experienced some of the problems likely to occur. In doing so he might gain something of the third factor (*pace* Hargreaves and Quicke). The innovator's status is important: Arends and Arends (1977) have suggested that your position in an organisation determines what you can know about it, and such knowledge might be necessary to particular types of innovation. Persons in high authority may never find out how others view them, yet they easily find out the external pressures on the system. Persons lower down may never understand the problems that their principals have at the system boundary. Having a certain position may facilitate or militate against various types of innovation. Within his own system a high-level person will possess authoritative power, i.e. he can direct others to undertake activities, and may also have greater access to rewards and powers of punishment than others lower down have. Innovative psychologists may have to find strategies for coping with routine casework – thus creating time for innovation – or work harder, possibly using their own time. Change usually requires extra energy and talent from the innovator over the period of transition.

Innovation Characteristics

Innovations with a problem-solving purpose are much more likely to result in success. Georgiades and Phillimore (1975) have indicated that:

1. one needs to 'cultivate the host culture' as an important first step;
2. a great deal of time is required, measured in years rather than months, to achieve change in an organisation;
3. one should work with those who are supportive of the project, rather than try to convert those against it in the organisation;
4. the target persons of the innovation should not be allowed to be isolated and unsupported;
5. the innovator should work with someone just below the top of the organisation — the person at the top must give permission for the project, but those just below him are often more supportive of innovation.

The innovation needs to be carefully planned, in execution as much as content. Curriculum development projects have often carefully prepared their materials, but spent less time and effort preparing the host school to accept and use the material (Dalin, 1973). This may well prove a greater problem than product development.

Arends and Arends (1977) have described an implementation strategy in which the local development of materials is a major component. They advocated that each school should take part in finding its own solutions 'even if it means reinventing the wheel'. Continuous planning, regular meetings with participants and provision for their extensive training were also suggested. One should be aware of the rewards and punishments operating on participants, and aim to maximise the reward element for steps achieved towards the innovation, for example by joint authorship of articles or papers on the project.

The scope of an innovation may be an important factor in its success. An innovation which affects the behaviour of many people involved in numerous subsystems will require a large input from the innovator and will risk more difficulties. Georgiades and Phillimore and Arends and Arends offer the same good advice: do not attempt a full frontal attack — no mass training or large-scale across-the-board activity. This would stretch the innovator's limited resources and the results would invariably be disappointing.

Factors Connected with the Innovator's Own Systems

External to the Innovator's System.   Innovation requires an enabling work-environment. This entails co-operation between a pioneer group of psychologists and enlightened administrators in a sympathetic authority. These constitute systems beyond the psychologists' own. To be included in this category are the local inspectorate, remedial teaching service and the client organisations (schools and headteachers, etc.).

In a survey of child guidance practice Bhattacharyya (1975) found much support for the notion of 'preventative work' (teaching, research, policy planning, etc.) amongst educational psychologists, *and also that the demands of referrals for individual casework prevented expansion of such work*. Topping (1979) in a study of his own local education authority found that headteachers still wanted psychologists to do individual casework, even though on the whole they considered it ineffective in changing the child. (It was effective, however, in reassuring the teachers.) Many of his psychologists were dissatisfied with the casework model, but only one worked in an alternative way, even though the service was tolerant of alternatives. Apparently restrictive high referral rates and long waiting lists may be themselves a part product of psychologists' own casework-oriented behaviour.

Within-system Factors.   By analogy with the findings of Georgiades and Phillimore on teacher training, newly qualified psychologists with innovative ideas might well undergo 're-education' at the hands of the first service for which they work. The new professional is likely to learn to perform work which gains the approval of his or her immediate boss. Working alone, using innovative skills which are not quite mastered, might be highly stressful for the lone innovative psychologist. Such factors could be catered for in an innovation-oriented organisation: the manager of change could protect such individuals by placing them in mutually supportive groups and shielding them from pressures from above and outside the organisation. On his own the lone innovator may suffer the same pressures as lone innovator teachers. The experience of the Ford Safari curriculum development project (Munro, 1977) suggests that the consequences for such a teacher are likely to be more work — and less popularity, promotion and self-confidence (the latter probably because performance worsens during a period of change, until one learns how to make the change and work up to potential).

Arends and Arends have suggested that innovators should work in teams of not less than two like-minded people. The multi-disciplinary, and therefore multi-theoretical, child guidance team has been the traditional group in which educational psychologists have worked. This may have tended to psychologists' working alone, or with only one or two other psychologists. Physical dispersal of psychologists between centres, working alone or in small groups, surrounded by personnel of varied theoretical outlooks, make it improbable that two like-minded psychologists will find themselves working alongside each other. It is more probable when a service has only one centre where its psychologists are concentrated, and especially where there is an appointment policy to attract new staff with similar theoretical positions. Forces which disperse psychologists reducing their frequency of contact and placing them in groups of theoretically electic personnel are likely to be counter-innovative. Quicke (1978) found that educational psychologists reported themselves largely 'eclectic', uncommitted to any one theoretical position but rather behaving without knowing or remembering from which theory their action was suggested.

At one extreme, therefore, innovative behaviour would be most unlikely from an eclectic psychologist, satisfied with current practice, with limited reading of the psychological literature, working as the lone psychologist in a child guidance team. It would be much more likely from a dissatisfied, widely read psychologist with a high contact with many other psychologists working in the same building in a service with low staff turnover and a high probability of meeting others with similar theoretical outlook and desire for change. It may be that innovation was low in the service that Topping (1979) studied because there were not enough factors operating to generate a 'critical mass'.

The would-be innovator must be prepared for in-built rewards and punishment structures to maintain the existing system of practice. Systems theory (Hodge, 1970) describes social systems as 'open', requiring an input of resources to maintain them. A characteristic of social systems, in contrast to closed systems, is that entropy or randomness decreases the more complex they become. They become more orderly, and the distribution of energy less random. Innovation may carry with it a risk of the unpredictable, and may therefore result in increased entropy. Managers of services (even psychological services) may want orderliness and predictability, and may act to reduce the chance of innovation by manipulating the factors described above.

The Target System of the Innovation

Innovation-overload is to be avoided. If a school has had a heavy dose of, for example, in-service training from another source (especially one involving a theoretical orientation different from that of the proposed innovation), likelihood of success may be reduced. This point overlaps somewhat with considerations of the scope of the innovation, but Georgiades and Phillimore have pointed out the pitfall of persuading a person or group to support an innovation, only to find they have not the power to sanction its implementation.

A Survey of Innovative Psychologists

Using the above categories a questionnaire was developed to explore possible supportive and constraining factors on the innovative behaviour of educational psychologists. First results appeared encouraging enough to report the preliminary findings here. Eight educational psychologists working in five child guidance centres in three local education authorities in the West Midlands were interviewed. Six psychologists were categorised as 'high innovators', because they showed continuous output of innovative work. Innovation was taken to mean 'a deliberate attempt to improve practice'. 'Low innovators' (two) were not characterised by continuous production: they had each undertaken only one isolated project. These preliminary findings appear to support the involvement of the previously mentioned factors, but also to identify others that discriminate between the high and low innovators.

Personal Factors

Dissatisfaction. Dissatisfaction with the 'traditional' educational psychologist role characterised all the high innovators.

Theoretical Position. High innovators had clear knowledge of the theories on which they based their intervention and professional actions. Behavioural psychology was strongly supported. They were certainly not 'eclectic' in the sense referred to by Quicke (1978).

Innovative Ideas. The innovative ideas of high innovators were more prolific and viable, and usually central to changing the role of psychologists — rather than being peripheral to it as were those of the low innovators.

Casework. High innovators saw casework as *not* their primary role.

Motive for Innovating. 'Giving away skills and psychology' or improving the service from psychologists were frequently given by high innovators as their motivation for innovating.

Exposure to Innovative Models. High innovators had often worked extensively with or taken part in other people's projects and innovations.

Area of Responsibility. An area of responsibility within the field of psychology had often been given or assumed by the high innovators. They had personal responsibility for the innovation.

Determination.   When asked the extent to which they would persevere with their innovation in the face of disagreement that was short of a request to stop from their principal, all the high innovators were clear that they would persevere, whereas the low innovators indicated they would stop their innovation.

Seeking Support.   High innovators tended to seek out the support of like-minded psychologists, whereas the low innovators did not, even though they were aware of the availability of such support.

Environmental Factors

High innovators tended to have at least one other psychologist as a partner in their project, who was equally or more dissatisfied with the traditional work of educational psychologists. This partner tended to have the same general theoretical position, or was strongly behavioural, or at least had the same theoretical orientation *vis-à-vis* the current project. The partner tended to work in the same centre, and was consequently someone with whom the innovator had frequent contact.

High innovators tended to have wider support from like-minded psychologists (i.e. those with similar theoretical positions, dissatisfied with traditional psychological work and undertaking innovative work). This support network ranged outside of the innovator's own centre often into neighbouring education authorities.

High innovators tended to have sophisticated casework-handling strategies, in contrast to the low innovators. They also had personal responsibility for the psychological service to a group of schools. Their case-handling strategies included prepared data-collecting forms, teaching programmes, and at one centre an extensive course for head-teachers introducing aspects of applied behavioural analysis and details of referral information required.

One low innovator had been contracted on a gentleman's agreement by the organisers of the Educational Development of the Young project to put on a training course following his own training in it. This contract had been a powerful condition enabling this psychologist to undertake his one innovation. It may well be possible to make more use of such a mechanism in university-sponsored innovation in education.

Two important functions of leadership have been described by Katz and Kahn (1978), task direction and psychological support, of which the former was missing in the environments of all the psychologists interviewed. Not one of the projects described was initiated by the principal psychologist of a local education authority. All were started as personal endeavours by the psychologist interviewed, and in all cases the principal provided only passive support for the project. Task direction as a function of the leadership role of principal psychologists is an area that should be examined in further research. It means getting a group of people to perform at acceptable levels, and involves co-ordination of the task of the group and offering of new approaches to the solution of problems. This implies a technical knowledge surpassing that of group members.

As major stresses at work, Katz and Kahn described role conflict, role ambiguity and overload. From the data so far highly innovative psychologists are at risk for all three, and perhaps therefore for stress illness too. Innovators are liable to find themselves doing their routine work in addition to their innovation. None of the psychologists interviewed had any concessions granted from routine work. Overload is thus a risk with which innovative psychologists are living. There are two types of overload, quantitative (too much to do in the time available) and qualitative (when the task is difficult to do). Social support (communication of positive affect, liking, trust, respect and affirmation of one's beliefs and perceptions) and some kind of direct assistance by significant other people in one's life, can reduce the effects of job stress. The social support system of the innovator within his own service and outside is an important consideration.

Towards a Theory of Innovation

It would be naive to suggest that these factors, personal and environmental, might if summed predict innovative behaviour on a simple correlational model. A model increasingly advanced in recent years for drawing together social data, and known for its facility in describing phenomenon in which continuous forces create discontinuous effects, is Catastrophe Theory (Zeeman, 1976). Such a theory would help to explicate the sudden onset (and falling off) of the innovative behaviour of a psychologist or a psychological service as variables in him and his environment altered. Future research and practice in this field might well consider such a model further.

Summary

This chapter has considered need for innovation by educational psychologists and some research into innovation in related fields, and described the preliminary findings of a survey of LEA psychologists. Further questions have been raised about the mechanisms and processes of innovation amongst educational psychologists. If no more one should be able to rate colleagues on the personal and environmental factors tentatively described in order to find those with whom it is most likely to be profitable to work, and suggest strategies for environmental engineering to foster innovations (Katz and Kahn, 1978, and Luthans and Kreitner, 1975, have described a number of technologies for organisational change). Bear in mind that a correlative model should be superseded by one that more realistically reflects the vagaries of the natural environment and social systems of work organisations.

5 CONSTRUCTING PSYCHOLOGICAL SERVICES IN SOCIAL SERVICES DEPARTMENTS

Barrie Brown

The professional context in which social services departments carry out their multifarious tasks is quite different in several senses from that operating in the national health service or in the local education authorities, in which clinical and educational psychologists respectively are employed. Any attempt to identify the long-term potential for developing psychological services in the context of social services departments should start out by examining those differences. Of the three state agencies dealing with social need, social services departments are the most under-resourced with trained professionals of any discipline. There are, for example, far more untrained residential and field social workers than there are untrained nurses in the national health service or untrained teachers in the local education authorities (RCA, 1977). Moreover, the social services departments, which were created by the Seebohm legislation of 1971, are the most recently formed. They are essentially an amalgamation of the old welfare and children's departments, together with some parts of the old public health departments. In common with area health and education authorities they are certainly large in size, mostly having in excess of 2,000 employees, with budgets running to many millions of pounds *per annum.* The central organising theme, however, developed by Seebohm and put into practice in the reorganisation of welfare services, is the prevention of overlapping of work, by the creation of a 'generic' training and mode of operation for social work. One social work profession provides services to all types of client groups and social workers are trained for generic work.

The scope of the responsibilities of social services departments are more extensive then either health or education. Put simply, they are the community agency with the primary responsibility for welfare for all persons between the ages of 0 and death. In practice these responsibilities include provision of day nurseries, residential nurseries, child care services including observation and assessment, children's and old people's homes, specialist hostels for the mentally ill, mentally handicapped and physically handicapped, day centres for various client groups and general fieldwork services.

Within the context of this complex range of tasks, reorganisation derived from Seebohm has yet to create a dominant professional group. There is, as yet, no parallel to the self-interested and protective professional power group evident in the health service and education authorities. Social workers are still in the process of creating the kind of power base from which doctors and teachers operate in those services. The process has perhaps been retarded because the actual organisational structure of social services departments is still remarkably fluid in the subsiding wake of the Seebohm reorganisation. Most departments are still searching for a mode of operation which maximises the quality and extent of services to client groups. It is in such a context that professional psychologists have yet to establish themselves, either numerically, or in complexity and impact of role. Of course, many graduate psychologists go on to become trained social workers and social work training includes a significant amount of theory and practice derived from the discipline of psychology. In using the term 'psychologist' in this chapter, however, the author is referring to graduate psychologists possessing a relevant postgraduate training in educational or clinical psychology, and employed in a job with the title 'psychologist'.

The following sections describe a variety of professional contributions which are being made by psychologists in social services departments for children, the mentally handicapped and the mentally ill. Psychologists also provide some services, of course, for the elderly and physically handicapped but these, as yet, are less well developed than for the other three client groups. It should be emphasised that little is known, yet, of the extent, scope or mode of employment of psychologists in social services agencies. Whilst there have been a number of descriptive reviews of the role of psychologists in these services (Bender, 1979a; Brown and Sawyer, 1978; Laishley and Coleman, 1978), there is little information about their mode of development and employment. These reports suggest that psychologists have much to offer to social services departments in their attempts to provide services for all client groups, and that the use of psychologists in these areas is changing rapidly. All that is attempted here is to give a broad overview of the context and kind of tasks which psychologists are offering. The chapter concludes with a review of future possibilities for the development of psychological services in social services departments.

Services for Children

Social services departments have a wide range of responsibilities for children as a client group, including observation and assessment centres, children's homes and community homes with education, to cater for the needs of children who require local authority care on a residential basis. Many authorities, too, have developed community-based alternatives to residential care — intermediate treatment and special family placement schemes — in an attempt to divert children from the residential sector or as an aid to their rehabilitation to the community. Social services departments also have responsibilities for children who are 'at risk', and are empowered through various legislative provisions to act in a preventative manner. Of particular interest in recent years has been the development of services for children at risk of 'non-accidental injury'.

At present the role of the psychologist in relation to services for children tends to be limited to the provision of psychometric assessments. In the main, such assessments are seen as part of the process of assessment which enables the social services departments to diagnose appropriately the problems of children seen to be in need. This role has perhaps been favoured by psychologists themselves (Edwardson, 1973) and certainly carries certain advantages. For example, it enables the psychologist to help residential care staff in children's homes, assessment centres and community homes with education to be more objective in their assessment procedures, and perhaps safeguard standards of administration of psychological tests in those contexts. In practice, however, the use to which psychometric data is put does not always remain within the control of the psychologist. The psychologist has no means for ensuring that recommendations and conclusions based on the collection of psychometric evidence are acted upon appropriately by other people, or indeed that his written report is used for its original purpose. At best, limiting the role of the psychologist to delivering the individual assessment service injects a degree of precision and apparent scientific rigour into the assessment of the needs of children in care, but such rigour and precision in the assessment process is wasted effort if neither the decision-making process nor the resulting recommended course of action is equally as precise. It rarely is.

Although it is rare for psychologists to be directly involved in a role expanded beyond individual assessment in social services department services for children, there are instances where such a role has been attempted and welcomed. Since 1975 a team of psychologists has been employed in the Birmingham area, seconded full-time from the education authority to the social services department, with a brief of providing services for the child care sector of the social services department, and based at Tennal Regional Assessment Centre. Over the years this team has become involved in many activities other than direct assessment. During 1977, for example, the authority wished to establish a special family placement scheme as a means of diverting some delinquent and disturbed children away from long-term residential care. The psychology team was asked to advise on the implementation of this scheme, and has been involved in selecting, supporting and evaluating foster parents and in identifying and following up children who might be placed appropriately in the scheme (Druce, 1977). Since 1976 psychologists in Birmingham have also been involved in the establishment and monitoring of a social-learning programme in a community home with education in the Birmingham area. The programme, based on a token economy, was developed in response to a need expressed by the head of the school to improve outcomes for delinquent boys placed in long-term residential care (Brown, 1977). Other development projects have included a social skills training programme and job preparation schemes for older delinquent youths.

Services for the Mentally Ill

Social services departments play a large part in helping those with mental disturbance or disorder, either to rehabilitate themselves from a psychiatric hospital back into the community or to remain in the community. Most local authorities have developed mental health social work teams whose specific task is to make provision for those who have received psychiatric help, and who require extra support to return to or remain in the community. Many authorities have opened day centres for this client group, catering for individuals who have been psychiatric in-patients or out-patients or for those in the community being treated by general practitioners, who might otherwise be moved into psychiatric hospital as in-patients. These day centres tend to offer personal and social support which is beyond the scope of existing facilities. In general, day centres and rehabilitative hostels have as their goal the prevention of further psychiatric breakdown with the provision of social, domestic and work skills support. In some instances they offer also group therapy, family casework and links with other community services. Both hostels for the mentally ill and day centres are staffed by people who are likely to have little experience in the mental health field and little specific training.

Psychologists appear to be involved rarely in the running, support and development of services for the mentally ill in social services departments. One notable exception is the service offered by the team of psychologists based in the London Borough of Newham (Bender, 1979a). This team has developed a policy of providing both psychological assessment and specific skills training and therapy services. The team of psychologists have focused on a psychiatric day centre, in which much effort has been devoted to developing psychometric and treatment skills in centre staff. Two day centre staff, for example, have been trained by the psychologists to conduct psychometric assessment. The centre includes a hostel where both assessment and treatment is available from a team of two residential social workers and one psychologist. This team meets weekly to discuss treatment goals and progress, and the psychologist may see clients and meet with the team as a group from time to time. This service has now developed away from the provision of treatment or assessment located within the centre of the hostel, and towards specific training for clients to survive successfully in bedsits and flats in the community. Consequently most of the input from psychologists is now focused on helping clients to acquire skills for living an independent life. Assessments are carried out on each individual client's ability to function independently in terms of self-care, social skills and ability to hold a job. Further assessment is carried out of the client's medical fitness and knowledge of welfare benefits by the psychologist and other members of the team, allowing for the development of an individual programme for that client, who is directly involved in assessing its relevance to his own particular needs.

Services for the Mentally Handicapped

Social services departments provide for the mentally handicapped as a client group mainly by placement in adult training centres and residential hostels. Area social workers work with families, but many training centres are increasingly providing family support. Hostels provide the largest number of residential places, but development of alternative and more independent living arrangements (for example, halfway houses and minimum supervision hostels, group homes, supervised lodgings, foster homes and so on) is accelerating rapidly.

These various trends in local authority provisions suggest that programmes integrating residential and day services are likely to be an
increasingly common feature. Although preventative techniques are
widely employed (e.g. at-risk screening, genetic counselling,
amniocentesis etc.), leading possibly to a gradual reduction in the
number of severely subnormal adults who are entirely dependent, it
is unlikely that the overall demand for services to the mentally
handicapped will diminish. The important factor here is the current
economic recession, making it harder for those in the borderline and
subnormal categories of mental ability and social competence to gain
and keep employment, and so to live independently without additional
training and support after leaving school. There is, therefore, likely to
be a continuing need to develop a range of services to span the short-
fall in provision between the levels of support currently available in
residential and educational resources and training which will encourage
complete independence in the community.

Adult training centres have in the past provided shelter, occupation
and recreation as well as a breathing space for caring relatives. There is
now, however, a trend in these centres to provide social education,
training in skills which are needed outside the day centre. There is
likely, therefore, to be a need to develop new skills in centre staff. It is
in helping social services departments to meet this need that psychologists perhaps have most to offer. For example, psychologists have
long been involved in the development of methods of assessment of
clients' needs in the health service, and have developed widespread
expertise in selecting training priorities and establishing goals of
treatment. The use of behaviour modification methods is particularly
relevant in this context in helping day centres to provide social
education, in particular behavioural-based methods of assessment of
base-line skills in an educational context in these settings is relevant to,
for example, the development of teaching programmes, curriculum
planning, skills analysis, continuous assessments, teaching aids and
resources and the assessment of alternative teaching strategies.

As well as working with clients and staff in community-based
agencies such as adult training centres, appropriate use of psychological
expertise with the mentally handicapped of the client group clearly
demands close co-operation by the psychologists with advisers, senior
managers and other helping agencies in the community (such as speech
therapists, physiotherapists, general practitioners and so on). Psychologists have the potential for acting as catalysts in promoting and
accelerating the shift from hospital-based services for the mentally

handicapped to community-based services. This catalytic role can be seen as an important bridging function between community-based units, such as adult training centres, and senior staff within the social services departments responsible for the many aspects of planning and decision-making which affect the nature and quality of the services. That is not to advocate that psychologists should set themselves up as yet another expert profession to work with the mentally handicapped, but rather as a support service to care staff, with the brief of helping them to develop their own procedures for assessment and to focus on problems objectively and systematically.

Problems of Implementation

This brief review of what psychologists are already doing in social services departments with three of the most numerous client groups suggests a wide range of tasks to which psychologists may address themselves. In the public eye, of course, psychologists are probably seen as those most qualified to administer and interpret individual tests of intelligence, personality and attainment, and to use such techniques to help other professional groups make appropriate diagnoses of the problem of the client. These are only some of the very broad range of skills possessed by qualified, professional psycho-logists. Psychologists can play a part in the process of assessment of the needs of many client groups in other ways, for example, by systematic observation, by collecting and collating information for other colleagues of other disciplines and by helping to set up systems for observation and data collection which are informative in plotting the effects of the specific interventions carried out by these disciplines. Psychologists are also skilled in a wide range of specific treatment methods, and are widely involved in the technical and clinical development of practice of this kind with adults and children. Equally, psychologists are well placed to offer advice and support to teachers and doctors, residential and field social workers, parents and staff working in various settings, offering help which they themselves can give to the client. Such consultative work needs to be conducted in a rigorous and sensitive way, of course, if it is to increase the effectiveness and skills of the professionals involved. Used appropriately, it may enable a wider dissemination of psychological techniques of intervention than could be implemented by the very limited number of psychologists currently employed in public service.

The problem facing the profession is not one of convincing other professional groups that they have something to offer. It is rather *how* they should be employed in social services departments, in what numbers and to perform what kinds of tasks. There are, for example, alternatives in the pattern of service input. Should psychologists provide services on demand from area managers and line management, or restrict their services to innovatory projects which operate for a finite period of time with a given and specific goal? Should psychologists attempt to provide a wide range of services to as many social services departments' resources as possible at one time, or focus on a limited number of projects in depth? Should services be provided directly to client groups, or focus on helping other professional groups to develop their own skills so as to provide a better service for clients? All these questions are relevant to the pattern of employment, accountability and responsibility of psychologists working in social services departments. In the absence of clear evidence of what works and what doesn't, there can be no clear answer to these questions. Perhaps by looking at some of the dimensions of difficulty which psychologists have already experienced in social services departments it may be possible to point to some considerations to which psychologists should address themselves as they seek to evolve a coherent and effective role.

The superordinate issue is to understand the organisational framework within which to develop a psychological service which makes maximum use of the skills of psychologists in collaboration with the other professionals involved. A useful framework perhaps is the one used by Bender (1976) — a multi-level approach of an expanded psychology service in whatever bureaucratic operation it is sited. Bender's three levels of operation at which psychological skills may be injected into the service have direct relevance to the organisation of the structure of social services departments:

1. working directly with clients either individually or in groups;
2. working indirectly with a larger group of clients by advising and supporting other staff groups such as teachers, residential social workers or nurses;
3. working with managers to monitor policy and planning and to engage in evaluative and action research.

Bender has postulated that if psychologists are to maximise their potential for influencing (for the good) the quality of life of the client groups that they relate to, in whatever bureaucratic context, they must work effectively and concurrently at all these levels.

There are many more examples of psychologists working at the first level in social services departments than at the other two levels. For example, Allen (1979) has provided a detailed example of how one social services department employed a psychologist to provide a home-visiting service for parents with pre-school mentally handicapped children. He focused on such aspects as the assessment of the development of self-help skills and describes how the role grew extensively during the years in which it was filled by a psychologist. Working directly with children in their homes enabled the psychologist to model a wide variety of methods for stimulating children, and helped other groups of workers (such as playgroup leaders and social workers) to understand better the various factors, social, emotional and neurological, which contribute to the individual child's failure to acquire particular skills. For Allen the questions raised by the experience of working in this way directly with social services departments concerned the limits of the role of a psychologist working at levels 1 and 2. In particular, he asked, should the psychologist become an integrated part of a fieldwork or a day and residential care service? For Allen the advantages of working at levels 1 and 2 were that an intense involvement with a number of families over an extended period was possible, that the experience of working alongside social workers in their work place opened up new vistas for the psychologist, and that the direct involvement of the psychologist with families and other professions out of the context of large-scale institutions, such as hospitals or schools, promoted the de-mystification of the psychologist. Similar justifications for the use of psychologists in levels 1 and 2 work have been made by Tully *et al.* (1978) in their description of work with agoraphobic clients in the community.

Whilst these two papers are not necessarily representative of the full range of work being carried out by psychologists currently in social services departments, they represent one manifestation of the broad dilemma that faces psychologists. There is clearly an enormous demand for clinical services to individual clients in a number of contexts. For example, Wheelan and Speake (1977) in their survey of adult training centres in England and Wales, noted that, out of 338 adult training centres, only 79 had indicated that they had a visit from a psychologist. Of the remainder, 165 centres said that they wanted to use psychologists to advise on educational programming and the quality of service that could be offered in the centres. Specifically they sought their counselling skills, objective assessment skills, programme-planning and behaviour modification skills, and openness to working with other professional groups. Only two of the centres indicated that they wanted less time than they were receiving: in the main psychologists were seen as second only to speech therapists in terms of the relevance of their skills for direct professional input into adult training centres.

The dilemma facing psychologists is, as Albee (1959) has indicated, that individual work with clients is insufficient in itself to disseminate widespread change in practice. Paradoxically the more successful the individual psychologist is in meeting the needs of individual clients within the context of a particular service, the more likely he is, after a period of time working at this first level, to want to negotiate for, and work towards, a greater influence. The pattern of progression in service from levels 1 to 2 and from 2 to 3 has perhaps been best demonstrated by the Newham group of psychologists. In 1971 when Newham Social Services Department (like the rest of the country) followed the recommendations of the Seebohm report and created a generic social work service, other professional groups were already involved in these services. Psychiatric social workers, for example, were working with individual neurotic clients in their offices. The psychologists, therefore, tended to focus their work more in day centres and hostels and, later still, developed links with field workers. The psychologist would not undertake individual assessment where there was little likelihood that the assessment would affect the outcome of treatment, because there were no alternatives available besides the one which the client was already using. It was only later, after this initial phase of working at level 1, that the psychologist began to develop specific projects to determine, to some extent, what the alternatives for treatment would be. The policy of the team was now to work with specified groups of clients with specific aims, working alongside groups of hand-picked staff who were also aware of the time and resource limits to the project. The goal of most projects was to help other professional groups develop skills so that psychologists could fade into a much more traditional consultant role allowing further projects to be developed. The team quickly found, however, that this project-based developmental role was itself ineffective in significantly increasing the dissemination of good practice in the day centres and hostels. Psychologists perceived that bad management and bad policy decisions were being made and that psychologists needed to be involved at a broader level on a consultant and advisory basis. Psychologists felt the need, for example, to get involved with staff appointments and to have a voice on the various planning committees (Bender, 1972; 1976).

The development of psychological services in social services departments from levels 1 to 3, from direct contacts to managerial advice and policy consultation functions, is likely, in other words, to encounter bureaucratic barriers. If, at the first level, the psychologist's inputs are effective, the line managers in day centres, residential hostels, community homes and so on (to whom the psychologist is responsible for providing the service) will become increasingly dependent on them and will tend to press for an expansion of this kind of service. The pressures on the individual psychologist are gradually to broaden his range of input at the first level, and he is soon likely to become overstretched. A common response to this pressure is to join with the line manager in pressing the authority for an extension of services through the appointment of a further psychologist. The more energetic and able the psychologist is at direct intervention, the more pressure there will be on him to expand, and consequently the less opportunity there will be for moving into the second level of input, indirect contact or skills transmission. Indeed, the psychologist who attempts to move into the business of staff support and development may well find himself in a role conflict with the manager who identifies that task as properly his own.

When he has developed the necessary conditions for moving into the second level of work (an explicit and trusting relationship with the line manager, and a clear understanding that level 1 work is likely to have less impact than level 2 work), further paradoxical pressures will exist for the psychologist attempting to move from the second level to the third level (from skills transmission to managerial advice and policy consultation), though in this case the precise nature of the pressures differs somewhat. Whilst sensitive and appropriate transmission of skills to other professional groups such as teachers and residential social workers tends to lead to pressure from managers to increase such input, the scope for development at this level tends to be limited by a short-fall in other support resources necessary for such development. Level 2 activities tend to demand a great deal of communication, both written and direct, between the psychologist and other professional groups. This not only creates pressures on secretarial and other support services (which are likely to be in short supply, in front-line social services establishments such as children's homes), but also there are likely to be demands from 'coalface' workers for definition of their responsibilities which may be at odds with the immediate requirements of the service. Level 2 activities with these groups of professional workers will require them to spend at least part of their working life reflecting on practice. Yet time and flexibility are likely to be as much in short supply as secretarial and back-up services. An example of this problem has been described by Brown (1977) with respect to problems faced by a psychologist in attempting to help a group of residential social workers in a community home with education to use token economy techniques.

If the role of the psychologist in a social services department is to expand beyond level 1 activities (such as assessment or interventive treatment), the barriers to stages 2 and 3 will need to be clearly recognised both by the psychologist and by the line managers with whom he works. Psychologists should also recognise that, whilst there is, as yet, no parallel in social services departments to the powerful vested interests in the health and education bureaucracies, what has been called a sense of vocation seems to be rapidly disappearing from social work. There is ample evidence in recent strike action taken by social workers in several authorities that as a professional group, they are becoming increasingly politically conscious. The disagreements of the sort between psychologists and psychiatrists in the health service over control of resources, accountability and clinical responsibility are still likely to be less overt in social services departments, but there can be little doubt that, as social work becomes more protective of itself, by virtue of its rapid development of training and the strengthening of the management structures, social workers are likely to start defining more precisely what they want from psychologists in much the same way as psychiatrists have done in the past.

These various considerations lead to a number of implications about the optimum organisation of psychological services to social services departments. If the psychologist has a role in helping the individual, in helping those who deliver primary care, and in advising on how to run and evaluate services, the profession should seek to integrate itself into the structure of social services departments vertically and horizontally. The only conceivable way to achieve this end will be for each social services department to have several psychologists working within it, so that they comprise a sufficiently large department, with a wide enough range of experience to encompass all three levels of input simultaneously. This will enable the psychologist to offset to some extent the bureaucratic barriers against the move from one level to another through support, protection and guidance from more senior colleagues. The overall development from levels 1 to 3 is likely to be expedited by clear objectives for the development of the psychologist's

role within the specified areas of the involvement, objectives which need
to be developed in collaboration with senior management within the
social services department. Most importantly, however, the psychology
service itself needs to be outside the executive management structure of
the authority in which it is working, so that lines of accountability for
the quality and evaluation of the psychologist's input can remain in the
hands of psychologists themselves rather than being syphoned off and
into the management structure. This is perhaps a particular problem at
the moment for those psychologists directly employed by social
services departments to work in regional assessment centres for children
where currently executive management responsibilities lie with the
head of the assessment centre, who also has responsibility for all other
aspects of management of the resource. This line manager is able,
therefore, to determine the direction, content and scope of the
psychologist's role. Because this perspective of that role may well be
intra-institutional, it can work against constructive development and
change within the institution, some consideration of which may be
stimulated by the psychologists. Furthermore if psychologists can
secure for themselves within social services departments a professionally
autonomous role, an active and discriminating referral system can be
operated rather than a passive one. This means that the psychologist is
in a position to negotiate with line management whether a task (be it
individual intervention, staff development or even policy planning) is
viable and relevant.

The model for the provision of psychological services in the social
services departments being suggested here is one which is unknown in
this country. Social services departments are only likely to be persuaded
that such radical developments are worth considering if psychologists
clearly underline what it is that they can offer which social services
departments need. Psychologists are after all relatively expensive
compared with home helps and meals on wheels, which in any case may
be seen as more basic services and more easily utilised. Whether
psychologists are worth the money, however, is obviously a political
issue rather than a rational one. What is common to all the emerging
isolated examples of existing input by psychologists to social services
departments is a broad-based, experienced and professional pool of
of expertise having its base in the academic core of knowledge of the
discipline of psychology. The profession has severe limitations in what
it can offer arising not least out of the irrelevance of much of postgraduate professional training in clinical and educational psychology to
the day-to-day needs of social services departments. What psychologists

can do, however, is to respond from a sound theoretical and clinical basis to specific questions about how services are to be planned in the best interests of clients, how they can be evaluated and how they can be delivered. What is lacking *now* for a realistic future development of the role of psychologists in social services departments on a broader basis than is currently available is general information about such basic facts as how many psychologists there are already working either directly with social services departments or on some kind of secondment arrangement, about their pattern of employment, what kind of tasks they are asked to undertake, to whom they are accountable or by whom given professional support or direction.

What psychologists are already doing tends to suggest that they have much to offer in the development and evaluation of services currently provided by social services departments. Given that these departments now have a massive task in meeting the needs of a wider and wider range of client groups, and have felt the need to develop an increasing variety of innovative methods of intervention, it seems an apposite time to examine closely ways and means of constructing psychological services in social services departments. This chapter has attempted to review some of the issues relevant to that task of construction.

6 SOCIAL SERVICES, PSYCHOLOGY ... AND PSYCHOLOGISTS

Andrew Sutton

Social services departments seem such an obvious happy hunting ground for psychologists that one might reasonably ask why psychologists were not much more fully involved in their work from the outset. Psychology itself occupies an important place in the much advocated professional training courses for social workers and residential staff; 'psychological problems', variously defined but usually involving the behaviour and development of clients, are central to many of the expressed concerns of social services departments; and Seebohm himself declared the personal social services to be 'large scale experiments in helping those in need'. At the same time the rapidly expanding professions of clinical and educational psychology have been looking for new arenas in which to exercise their desire to work with wider ranges of problems 'in the community'. What could appear more rational and for the public good than that the mushrooming new social services departments, community-based, dealing with a huge range of unresearched problems of an apparently psychological nature, by their very nature innovative and eager to 'experiment' with new forms of provision, should turn to psychologists, eager for the insights and techniques that they might contribute to their work? Things are not always as they seem, however, and the social services departments have made no general attempt to draw psychologists into their work, except in their processing of children through the juvenile justice system. Indeed there are not a few psychologists who have found their own overtures to social services departments soundly rebuffed over this period.

Local authority social services departments as presently manifest are but one stage in a long process of historical development, one which will presumably continue on into further phases. The relationship between psychologists and social services and its possible future development are more explicable in the light of wider historical developments of which 'social services' in the 1970s have been but a part, and of the place and meaning of 'psychology' in that development.

The Rise (and Fall?) of Professional Social Work

An attractive and immediate interpretation of our present system of local authority welfare provision is a teleological vision of continuous and progressive reform, in which the two strands of increasingly humane concern for the client and greater professional skill have intertwined to culminate in our present social services departments. Project this view into the future for a prospect of even greater and more widespread 'care' and yet higher levels of 'professionalism', in which psychologists will have much to offer and with which they should be proud to associate. There are, however, other possible interpretations, other aspects that require emphasis. Above all there is the close association of social services and social work with poverty and the poor.

Administering the Poor Law

Jordan (1974) has argued in great detail the prime historical association of poverty with our present services. The essence of his analysis is that there is

> . . . a remarkable persistence of the very oldest principles derived from the first Poor Law, and a tendency for the newer, more shallow-rooted products of democratic compromise (like the insurance principle) to be assimilated into the old system and ultimately relegated to a subsidiary role, at least in relation to the group which has traditionally received most attention from the social services. Above all, there is a strong tendency for these old principles to reappear in new guises as successive governments employ the social services as means to accomplish their traditional tasks of reinforcing the work ethic, maintaining the sense of family responsibility, and keeping law and order.

From this viewpoint poor relief, state intervention in family life and public order are but different aspects of a single policy commitment which have recombined in different ways at successively high levels since the feudal period ended. Two basic principles especially were apparent even in the Poor Law Act (1598).

1. The principle that the poor should wherever possible be maintained by their own families. This early means test has largely excluded the middle classes and the better-off employed, not only from poor

relief but also from uninvited state intrusion into their personal
lives. The principle bears the obvious corollary that those who can
work should.
2. The need to prevent the poverty of the poor and the personal and
social evils associated with it from becoming a threat to society.

By the end of the eighteenth century inflation and the fear of
revolution on the French model had lead to a policy of subsidising the
wages of low-paid agricultural workers on a scale related to the size of
their families and the price of bread. This, and perhaps also the
advantages to both manufacturers and poor law overseers of the cheap
labour of poor-house children (Pivan and Cloward, 1972), encouraged
the poor to have large families as a way of qualifying for poor relief.
This policy was widely regarded as 'demoralising' the poor and 'creating
an army of paupers': it also offended against the quality of family life
and failed to contain the unrest of the rural poor. It was reversed by
the Poor Law Amendment Act (1832), the effects of which are
probably most widely known through the pages of *Oliver Twist*. The
new act abolished the allowances that had encouraged large families:
in future failure to provide was to be punished, not rewarded, and the
test of need was to be the offer of admission to the workhouse where
conditions were to be 'less eligible than those of the independent
labourer of the lowest class'. The bond between family members was
used as a means of enforcing the principle of independent maintenance
from work and wages: in the workhouses husbands were separated
from wives, parents from children. The alternative to the workhouse
was labour at humiliating tasks under strict discipline and conformity.
    Though not universally employed with the same rigour the
'principles of 1834' continued to be quoted and asserted well into the
twentieth century. One of these principles was that poverty is a moral
problem, a question of choice, and constitutes a depravity that should
be confined to as small as possible a group of incorrigibles, thus saving
from contamination a larger class of persons who were poor but
industrious. This conception of an 'undeserving' and a 'deserving' poor
clashed, however, with a growing factual knowledge about the material
causes of poverty. Widows and orphans, for example, were found to
claim relief largely because their menfolk had died from infections and
fevers: their destitution was therefore a question of public health and
hygiene rather than moral turpitude. At the same time seasonal
unemployment created bitter poverty for men who would much rather
work, and would rather die than commit their families to the

workhouse. Such deserving cases could increasingly find 'voluntary relief', charitable money distributed quite apart from the Poor Law authorities. The charities made a clear distinction between those who were 'reduced to distress without fault or improvidence of their own', whom they sought to help, whilst urging that the official system of poor relief should be made 'as distasteful as possible' for those whom they did not (Charity Organisation Society, 1870). Lloyd-George's insurance scheme introduced before the Great War made the state responsible for the deserving poor, the thrifty members of the working class, though the institutions of the Poor Law still continued for the less provident. The mass unemployment of the twenties and thirties, however, brought the 'principles of 1834' into conflict with the need to maintain law and order. Webb (1948) pointed out that

> . . . the abolition of relief, except under penal conditions, not only increased mass destitution, with its inevitable mendacity and vagrancy, but as many witnesses asserted, actually multiplied the number of criminals; the energetic and self-willed man preferring a life of theft and fraud, with its off-chance of prison, to the certainty of daily existence in one of the able-bodied 'test' workhouses . . .

The inter-war years saw a gradual acceptance of the inappropriateness and failure of the workhouse system, and from 1934 onwards the Employment Assistance Board provided at least a means-tested outdoor relief without the workhouse test. After more than a century the destitute could again apply for poor relief without fear of grim institutionalisation for themselves and their families.

The Second World War, with the temporary sense of national unity and purpose that it engendered, brought the Beveridge Report (1942), the 'British Revolution', incorporating universalistic principles that intended identical social services for *all* who were deprived of a normal decent family life, whatever the reason and whatever their place in society and without enquiry into whether or not they were 'deserving'. It was not that poverty and pauperism ceased to exist, but rather that maladjustment and emotional hazards existed at all levels of society, not just amongst the demoralised and undeserving at the bottom, and were therefore the appropriate targets for services established on universalist principles to serve rich and poor alike. The One-Nation idea of the original Welfare State, however, contained a fundamental flaw which left the door open for the old distinctions, the inability of the National Insurance Scheme to deal with more than *interruptions* of earnings, and the consequent need to maintain a separate provision (by way of the National Assistance Board) for those poor people whose dependence was *permanent*. Growing affluence lead to a desire to link national insurance with wages rather than prices, achieved first through 'contracting out' and then through earnings-related state benefits, with increasing differentials between the benefits received during unemployment by better-off workers, and those of the poorly paid. With the 'rediscovery of poverty' in the mid-sixties it was found that two-fifths of the households living below National Assistance level were primarily dependent upon earnings (Townsend and Abel-Smith, 1965). The Ministry of Social Security Act (1966) established an apparent right to Supplementary Benefit, but it was not an *absolute* right dependent upon contributions (as in the National Insurance Scheme). Without such an absolute right the concept of undeservingness crept back, manifest in social and official attitudes towards the voluntarily unemployed ('scroungers'), and in administrative sanctions such as the curtailment of benefits. Against a background of increasing vigilance against fraud the supplementary benefits system has involved an increasing number of claimants, thereby denying Beveridge's strategy that the insurance principle should be the prime means of providing social security, and restoring the concept of relief. Beveridge's plan was finally killed off in the seventies by the deepening crisis in the economy and the approaching problem of life-long unemployment that has been our major societal response to date to the new technological revolution. As at the end of the eighteenth century the outcome was a new class of subsidised paupers, dependent for their livelihood upon Supplementary Benefit and Family Incomes Supplement.

This new 'army of paupers' enters the eighties with substantial detachments of the old, the chronically sick and handicapped, single-parent families, low-income groups, the unemployed, black youth and jobless school-leavers generally. It does so under the prospect of recession and deindustrialisation, most immediately manifest in 'The Cuts' in the public services which had expanded over the seventies to meet their stated welfare 'needs', and a massive new emphasis on 'Law-and-Order'. It could be that we are indeed 'in the process of a deep and decisive movement towards a more disciplinary, authoritarian kind of society' (Hall, 1980).

The Professionalisation of Social Work

The present local authority social work profession springs from several divergent historical traditions. The oldest of these is the tradition of casework and care, largely deriving from the voluntary relief societies; the second is 'scientific' professionalism, largely from psychiatric social work; the third is managerialism, largely a phenomenon of social work's recent involvement as an agent of local government.

The Voluntary Societies.   The Charity Organisation Society had been founded in 1869 as an attempt to rationalise the activities of the vast array of charitable organisations tending to the poor. The Society asserted that random and unco-ordinated charity served merely to encourage abuse and thereby acted to produce a class of dependent mendicants, particularly in the big cities where the problem was exacerbated by the physical (and therefore personal and moral) separation of the social classes. By means of careful and systematic record-keeping social casework would control multiple approaches to charitable bodies, and all such approaches would be funnelled through district offices. The casework method involved not just personal contact and friendship with the poor, but also a degree of surveillance and control of beneficiaries. Concern over the widening gap between the social classes in the cities was the basis of another wing of rational or 'scientific' charity, the Settlement Movement. The university settlements were initially established in the latter part of the nineteenth century to bring knowledge to the lower classes: some, however, soon found themselves involved in a secondary function. The university women who worked in the settlements, finding their way into the established professions largely blocked, saw the possibility of a new career opportunity in professional social work to be created away from male domination. University settlements began to co-operate with the Charity Organisation Society in setting up professional training courses in social work. By the end of the century a small but strong tradition was emerging of personal service and professional training, largely involving middle-class women. Almoning in the voluntary hospitals and dispensaries, where an important task was to sort those who could pay from those who could not, was an early offshoot. This tradition was already separate from two quite distinct sectors of concern for the plight of the poor, that also had common roots in voluntary, charitable effort. Middle-class men who had been drawn into the Settlement Movement found readier career outlets in politics, where economic analyses discounted social work in favour of social administration, while the respectable working-class men who had comprised the majority of court missionaries were more concerned with their terms of service, and began to establish formal links with the state (see Parry and Parry, 1979).

The 'Psychiatric Deluge'.   The Charity Organisation Society had
advocated 'scientific' social work, but its legitimation remained
religious rather than secular, and its science was little more than
'bureaucratic rationality' (Parry and Parry, 1979). Psychiatry offered
not only a legitimation but also a method, a new place of work and a
whole new clientele. Psychiatric social work had its origins in the
United States where the enormous inrush of psychiatric (more properly
'psychoanalytic') ideas into social work is known as the 'psychiatric
deluge'. Sheldon (1980) has quoted a contemporary account.

> Atlantic City in 1919 was a landslide for Mental Hygiene: the
> conference was swept off its feet. In every section psychiatrists
> appeared on the programme. The Psychiatric Social Worker was
> present in person for the first time and violent indeed were the
> discussions which raged about her devoted head — what should be
> her training, what her personality, and what the limitations of her
> province? Should she remain for ever different from other case
> workers or should every other case worker be reborn in her likeness?
> This was the meeting which burst its bounds and had to be
> transferred to a church a block away. Dignified Psychiatrists and
> Social Workers climbed out of windows in order to make sure of a
> good seat.

There seem to have been no similar scenes in this country, in Sheldon's
terms the steady inroads made by the psychiatric approach being more
a 'drizzle' than a deluge. This occurred largely through the spread of
the Child Guidance Movement in the late twenties and early thirties,
which in England (though not in Scotland) fell from its outset under
the control of psychiatry (and therefore mental health models and
psychoanalysis) rather than psychology (see Keir, 1952). Psychiatry
offered more than an apparently scientific knowledge base. It offered
also the glamour and prestige of association with psychiatrists and a
range of clients across the social spectrum, rather than the image of the
social worker concerned only with the poor, with charity and
evangelism, and with cranky local dignitaries. By the end of the thirties
there were more than 40 child guidance clinics in England and Wales,
many voluntary, but some significantly founded by the state in the
form of local authorities. When the British Federation of Social
Workers was formed in 1936 as an umbrella organisation for twelve
separate social work bodies, the psychiatric social workers exercised an
influence out of all proportion to their numbers, holding up a model

of professionalism that was not just trained, but also scientific in its knowledge base and universalist in its application.

Local Authority Social Work.   The national unity of the Second World War brought legislation to do away with inequality and poverty. If poverty were to disappear, then a poverty-oriented social work would go with it: on the other hand a social work directed to psycho-social needs would find enormous scope in the new universalist provisions. The new local authority departments, welfare, mental welfare and children's, had inherited an appalling legacy: the National Assistance Board took all responsibility for outdoor relief, leaving the local authorities the institutional side of the Poor Law to administer. Despite this the children's departments, created by the Children's Act (1948) and the most progressive of the new local authority departments, created both a new breed of *public* social workers and provided a model of social workers managing their own local government departments. In the welfare departments with their larger caseloads and more narrowly defined tasks Poor Law traditions lingered on (Jordan, 1974). Over the fifties and sixties the children's departments especially absorbed the ideas of casework of a 'psychological' nature, to which the social work elite was still wedded, and integrated them into their practice. The casework ideology was proselytised through the growing number of professional training courses, the idea of a unified knowledge base having its reflection in the idea of a unified profession of trained social workers. At the same time work with 'problem families' brought the departments into conflict with what they regarded as the inflexible and less understanding attitudes of the National Assistance Board officers in dealing with what the latter tended to regard as feckless and undeserving behaviour. Out of casework, therefore, there sprang a desire to provide financial assistance, and the Children and Young Persons Act (1963) included the provision for children's departments to give 'assistance in kind, or in exceptional circumstances, in cash'. Casework became embroiled once more in poor relief, though the old traditions of deservingness were restated: applicants for services now ran the risk of being treated as 'inadequate' or 'maladjusted'. Perhaps significantly, when the goal of a unified local authority social work agency was achieved administratively by the Social Services Act (1970), more chief officers from the small, rather backward welfare departments became directors of social services than did those from the larger casework-oriented children's departments.

    The new social services department social worker was a hybrid, not only in the diversity of traditions that fed into the new profession but also in the very basis of that professionalism. Despite the pretensions of professional training the local authority social worker was not an autonomous professional: nor was (s)he wholly a creature of the bureaucratic hierarchy. The social worker's status represented a negotiated partnership between social work, which wanted to be 'a profession', and the state, which required managers and organisers. Social workers were to be 'bureau-professionals', a status which at least promised the chance to offer professional skills within a humanised bureaucratic structure (Parry and Parry, 1979). Over the course of the seventies, however, the apparent triumph of professionalism proved short-lived. The old social work elite held little sway in the new social services departments, either amongst senior staff, many of whom came from other traditions of social work, or amongst the legions of new entrants, many of whom were more interested in trade unionism than in professionalism. There were more trained personnel, but also wider responsibilities and tasks, especially following the Children's Act (1969), and a growing dissatisfaction with the shaky (even non-existent) knowledge base of social work. This dissatisfaction was increased by the political orientation of many of the new social workers, who sought *social* interpretations and solutions to the problems of the poor, rather than psychological approaches, alienating them not only from their own professionalism but also from the goals and ideologies of their employing institutions. The social services departments' response to the moral panic over child abuse was almost wholly procedural and bureaucratic, rather then professional and scientific (see Howells, 1974), perhaps indicating the degree to which the previous ideals have been abandoned. The control of the system has shifted from social workers to bureaucrats, from women to men, and it is not unreasonable to state that local government social work is undergoing an acute crisis of self-confidence. An example of the disillusion within social work itself with its professional knowledge base, and the aversion to the procedures that cover this lack of knowledge, has been provided by Didrichsen (1979), in respect to social work with cases of child abuse.

How can such preventitive work be operated? At the moment there is no behavioural science that can predict with certainty peoples' future behaviour . . . Nevertheless many agencies involved in child care produce publications which imply that such knowledge is available . . . Using this framework, social workers have not been

able to deal with the problems, and the employment of increased
numbers of them does not logically imply a solution to the problem
. . . The answer to the problem is then seen in increased supervision,
monitoring of families, increased vigilance towards the phenomenon
by the public, increased investigation, etc. . . . It is important to
realise that the people at the receiving end of the preventative work
have not broken any laws, battered any children, nor, in most cases
even asked for help with their problem.

Responses to this disillusion, both from within social work and without
(see Sutton, 1981) have included the recommendation that social work
abandon all pretence both to 'care' and to technical interventions into
human affairs, and aim instead at an honest, humane and efficient
administration of the system.

Social Workers' Psychology

Despite widespread disillusion, however, the majority of social work
institutions (both employing and 'professional') remain firmly
committed to 'psychological' understandings of the problems facing
them, and there are still very many individual 'believers', social workers
who hold fast to the old beliefs. There are after all powerful structural
encouragements for explanations of poverty that depend upon
personal, rather than economic factors, and whilst moral turpitude has
lost its credibility, the 'cycle of disadvantage' (Joseph, 1972) serves to
focus attention upon individual rather than societal imperfections.
Many of the new generation of social workers are too sophisticated to
accept mentalistic explanations of the problems that face them in their
daily work, yet the constraints of their jobs allow them little alternative
in many instances: they must either act on that model, or get out.

The Old School

Social work has no explicitly formulated knowledge base, indeed it has
no knowledge base of its own at all, drawing widely in its professional
training from social administration, sociology, and a variety of fields
which might very loosely be regarded as 'psychological'. The central
contradiction of social work is that it has been 'singular among the
disciplines, claiming a professional status in the absence of a knowledge-
base' (Bitensky, 1978). It is a calling without a communicable core of
knowledge. Further, it should be noted, the fields that it draws from

are largely American. The professional training for British *public service* social workers draws heavily from the literature of American social work, and also fairly widely from what in the United States are called psychotherapy and counselling. A substantial proportion of the American literature derives from private practice, with quite different social classes represented in its case-load, and a quite different degree of professional autonomy than in the case of the British local authority social work. In seeking the psychology that is transmitted to our social workers in their professional socialisation one must therefore be prepared for an unformulated and amorphous body of knowledge, with perhaps little apparent relationship to the demands of their practice. One must also be prepared for a very different understanding of the word 'psychology'. To most psychologists it presumably retains its primary meaning of the scientific study of human thinking, develop-ment, behaviour, etc. (whilst most psychologists would be prepared to dispute amongst themselves over the latter part of such a definition, few would quibble over the former). To many social workers, however, perhaps to most, it is the secondary, informal or colloquial meaning of the word 'psychology' that assumes primacy, its use to connote 'the mental make-up of people that causes them to act as they do'. Above all, it is about 'feelings'.

Psychoanalytic theories, often in vitiated form (see Morgan, 1975), are still a component of many social work training courses, where they occupy an important place in understanding child development (often co-existing incongruously with separate courses on sociology and on behaviour modification). Theories are taught without the concept of experimental test, and the student is left with the impossible task of forming his or her own personal synthesis according to personal preferences or pressures within the given course. Without the concept of experiment there can be no objective test of rival theories, and no evaluation of the resultant practices. The social worker's 'psychology' is rich in ideas, and very thin indeed on demonstrable techniques.

Denied a clear concept for psychology (other than that it must somehow be important) the social worker may then be left to make it up as (s)he goes along. The culture of the area office and the expecta-tions of other professions may well influence the social worker to attach great value to such matters as 'insight', 'threat' and 'relationships'. The social worker's own supervision by the senior or team leader may be conducted in these terms, providing a most powerful force for continuing socialisation into this ethos for those amenable to it. As a result the social worker's professional expertise may turn out to comprise no more than a tangled mass of professional ideology, common assumptions and personal experiences and prejudices (see Sutton, 1981; 1980a).

Presumably a further legacy from the 'psychiatric' background of professional social work is the continuing emphasis upon 'assessment' or 'diagnosis' and upon 'treatment'. The by now extensive (and uniformly unfavourable) American literature on effectiveness research in fields analogous to British social services work has been reviewed by Fischer (1978): the limited British literature closely parallels this (Sutton, 1981). Especially in the field of child care the social work establishment has made enormous claims of professional competence, and has received wide-ranging authority over clients' lives and a substantial share of public resources in return. The claims to expertise were premature, and the practical results are now increasingly apparent. The clients were the first to notice it. Before the Children's Act (1969) children in Approved Schools up and down the country used to sing to the tune of *Old Smokey*, a song that they had borrowed from Borstal Trainees

> The judge said sit down boy/girl,
> And dry up your tears.
> You're going to approved school,
> Six months to three years.
> So kiss me my darling
> And say you'll be mine,
> You're going to approved school
> For a hell of a time.
>
> I counted the moonbeams,
> I counted the stars,
> I counted one hundred
> Of these prison bars.
> Now I have done one year,
> And one year's to do.
> I'll get out of this place
> If it's the last thing I do.

> (from a collection by Janet Read)

Children in 'community homes with education' no longer sing this song. 'Treatment' is indeterminate, and there is no way of knowing or counting off a sentence. A new generation of liberal pressure groups has now arisen (Justice for Children, Family Rights Group), opposed to the potential injustices of a system of compulsory treatment at the hands of fallible 'experts'.

New Waves

Amongst social workers and other social services personnel one reaction to the increasingly apparent failure of their professionalism has been a disillusion with psychology. Another has been to seek new psychologies. Over the last decade two altogether separate different approaches have been looked to. Again, both are largely transatlantic in origin, and again, because of the catholicity of social work, it is possible to find both approaches co-existing, apparently without stress, within the ideas of a single professional.

The 'radical' or 'alternative' approach to psychology in social work may be epitomised by the sources presented in a counter-course for social work students (SCANUS, 1976). Essential readings recommended to link psychology with social control were the writings of Reich, Laing, Fanon and Freud, 'who each contribute important elements towards an understanding of the psychology of oppressed social life'. In the section on 'psychology, psychiatry and child development', Goffman was recommended for his classic study of asylums, and Szasz for his critical essays on psychiatry. So too was Fromm for an up-to-date critique of Freud; Berne, for games people play; Janov, for primal screams; Rogers, for encounter groups; Perls, for Gestalt Therapy; and perhaps surprisingly Köhler, for Gestalt Psychology. The study of Reich was also recommended. A much larger section on the 'experiential sciences' was largely devoted to the works of Laing, Cooper and their commentators, which expressed a reaction to 'the established behavioural schools of thought in psychology, psychiatry and sociology'. Though the works of the writers suggested in the counter-course, along with those from other sectors of the Personal Growth Movement, have certainly contributed to the thinking and life-style of many social services entrants, there are as yet no clearly documented effects of such ideas' having any discernible effect upon local authority practice.

On the contrary it was behaviourism and the various practical techniques stemming from it that emerged as a discernible new force within social work at the end of the seventies. Within social work itself, in fieldwork, in day care and in residential provision, there are those who would seek to behaviouralise social work. Social services workers are urged to join the British Association for Behavioural Psychotherapy and the Association for Behaviour Modification with

Children, and a Behavioural Social Work Group has been recently formed. And almost for the first time there are psychologists with a common and explicit approach, apparently eager to share their skills to generate new forms of practice (e.g. Brown, 1978a). Perhaps we are now set for a steady 'behavioural drizzle' in social work.

The Psychologists

The history of psychology is much shorter than that of the Poor Law, shorter even than that of voluntary social work, though child psychology antedated the introduction of psychiatric social work and its psychoanalytic orientation into this country. Until recently, however, psychologists' contact with the issues presently dealt with by social services departments have been slight. Burt (1925) took an early interest in delinquent children, their investigation and upbringing. He advocated a detailed investigation of the individual child and of his physical and social circumstances, and a careful check upon the effects achieved by any treatment recommended. Much of the former seems implicit in present-day social services assessment procedures (though many modern practices in this field fall short of Burt's suggestions): his experimental approach is not apparent. Burt's work seems now largely forgotten in social work circles, and whether it has indeed had any direct, linear influence on present-day practices remains to be documented. In England and Wales (though not in Scotland) the educational psychologists who went to work in the new child guidance clinics from the late twenties onwards found themselves in the main under psychiatric domination, their functions 'limited to the cognitive aspects of the mind, i.e. the application of intelligence and educational tests, together with the coaching of children who present specific difficulty in any school subject' (Keir, 1952). Psychology as a whole comprised only a small workforce, clinical psychology had yet to emerge as a discrete entity, and the psychiatric deluge assured those within social work that all was well in their world as far as professional theory and technique were concerned. There was little change until the major expansion of the social services departments and of psychology in the seventies.

Educational Psychologists in Observation and Assessment Centres

Over the sixties and into the start of the new decade four local authority departments (later social services departments) established their own psychological provisions, though only one of them, in Newham, survived the major local government reorganisations that followed. In the mid-seventies, however, the enlarged local education authorities' school psychological services undertook the routinised provision of reports to the juvenile courts, this becoming a regular practice in most, perhaps all local authorities. Their provision is made through the courts departments and assessment services of the social services departments. On the basis of a recent national survey of educational psychologists in England and Wales (Wedell and Lambourne, 1979) it may be estimated that around 200 educational psychologists now visit social services departments' observation and assessment centres, mainly for the purposes of providing psychological reports for the courts. Their efforts represent not only the major input by psychologists into the English judicial system, they also comprise a massive contribution of psychologist-hours to the routine child care work of social services departments. Despite the scale of their work there has been little examination of what they actually do there (for further details see Moss and Sutton, 1980).

There are a variety of ways whereby a psychologist might find himself reporting upon a child or family involved with a social services department, or working on the operations of a social services establishment, but the routine provision of psychological assessments to observation and assessment centres has probably been the major single point of contact. The Children and Young Persons Act (1969) had stipulated that every regional plan for child care should include proposals

> . . . for the provision of facilities for the observation of the physical and mental condition of children in the care of the relevant authorities and for the assessment of the most suitable accommodation and treatment for these children.

The local authorities' interpretation of this requirement has been largely the establishment of residential *centres* where children are 'observed and assessed'. The Association of Educational Psychologists (1976) has proposed that 'One of the most specific requirements [of the 1969 Act] is that children who are made the subject of Care Orders should have their personal needs assessed by a multi-disciplinary team which includes a psychologist.' The two interpretations have perhaps more in common with each other than with the Act.

Despite educational psychologists' extensive commitment to work

in observation and assessment centres there has been only one account
of how they might proceed in such work. Edwardson (1973) offered
early guidelines for practice according to a school which may (perhaps
unfairly) be summarised as a little testing, a little common sense and a
lot of consultation. Psychometrically dependent approaches persisted
in a major course on psychologists' work for social services departments
organised by the Division of Educational and Child Psychologists of
the British Psychological Society in 1978 (see Moss and Sutton, 1980).
Opposition to the whole concept of 'observation and assessment',
particularly its residential form, has been advanced only by Cooper
(1975; 1976); Brookes (1977) has enthusiastically supported it,
Clayton (1979) would like the observation and assessment, but without
its residential aspect. There seems reason (see Sutton, 1981) to regard
the primary purpose of observation and assessment centres to be
structural to the child care system, rather than dependent on either
the requirements of the 1969 Act or on the 'needs' of the children
(however defined). It is hard not to view the wholesale involvement
of educational psychologists in these centres as structural to the needs
of their own professional systems rather than dependent upon, say, the
unique contributions that a psychologist might make to problems of
observing and of assessing children, or upon the psychological
evaluation of the validity of residential procedures.

As far as one can tell (Brown and Sawyer, 1978; Moss and Sutton,
1980) the role filled by many educational psychologists in the observation and assessment centres has been mainly psychometric and
legitimating. By 'psychometric' is meant the administration of intelligence and reading tests, and the interpretation of the child's behaviour
under test to explain wider aspects of his life. By 'legitimating' is
meant: first, the provision of a nominally independent expert opinion
to back up the individual recommendations of the observation and
assessment centre; and secondly, reassurance that all is well in what is
being done, simply from the active collaboration of yet another
'expert' in the system. There may exist, perhaps in considerable
numbers, educational psychologists who have undertaken innovative
psychological work and made significant changes in their local
observation and assessment systems, if so they have yet to publish their
work. There are certainly educational psychologists who have been
grossly dissatisfied with the constraints upon their own work at such
centres and with the quality of the 'observations' and 'assessments'
made there, and have withdrawn from the work altogether. And there
are certainly educational psychologists who have taken a third course:

unable or unwilling either to innovate or withdraw, they have stayed on, producing mediocre work or even outrightly bad psychological practice. Psychologists who deprecate the 'psychology' of certain social workers that they meet, or wonder at the antipathy or suspicion that they themselves meet from many others, should remember that the most substantial contact that social services departments have yet had with psychologists has been with a branch of psychology which has shared some of the recent professional problems of social work itself. Educational psychology, too, has had to establish itself as 'a profession' within local government (Sutton, 1976), and within the compromise of its own bureau-professionalism it has perhaps been experiencing its own recognition of the progressive supremacy of managerial over scientific considerations.

Other Psychological Research and Practice

Five years ago very little indeed had been published to link psychologists with the work of social services departments. Suddenly, however, there is a growing literature. The following overview is not intended to be exhaustive, but to illustrate the particular directions taken by this sudden upsurge of interest.

General Social Services Work.   The psychology service within the social services department of the London Borough of Newham is the only one of four early services to have survived the reorganisation of the early seventies. Despite widespread proselytisation of its principles (see for example Bender, 1972; 1976; 1979b) it has remained a solitary phenomenon. It was established originally as a clinical psychology service for adult mental welfare cases, and accounts of its activities remain unique amongst published work for their prime focus upon a range of adult problems, psychiatric cases, mental and physical handicap and the elderly. Its status as a psychological service wholly within a social services department, linked neither with the education authority's school psychological service nor with an outside research agency, also remains unique. Whether it can in any way be construed as providing 'community psychology', as is often claimed for it, remains a matter for debate. A less partisan evaluation of a social services department's possible requirements for psychologists has been offered by Shackleton-Bailey (1979) who based his study on the possible needs of Hampshire Social Services Department. His main examples of areas of possible contribution by psychologists to the department's work are with mentally handicapped adults and the adult 'mentally ill', the

omission of work with children being of note in a county known for
its powerful schools psychological service. His advice to social services
departments, as potential employees of psychologists, is measured.

> How should a County like Hampshire proceed? The first answer
> must be: cautiously! To identify a need and to employ people to
> meet that need guarantees nothing. Other members of the Social
> Services team will be the main consumers and they would be well
> advised to test the soup before taking a large swallow. The
> effectiveness of psychological help and methods would have to be
> carefully assessed; it would be unwise to rely entirely on
> psychologists' own job descriptions.

Brown and Sawyer (1978), Brown (1979) and Porteous (1979) have
outlined some of the ingredients for the psychological soup to be fed
mainly to children in care. A range of recipes has been provided by
Williams (1979).

Mental Handicap.   Gray (1979) has penetrated social services work
in a quite contrary way. He works not as 'a psychologist', but in a 'real'
job, as the manager of an adult training centre in Great Yarmouth.
Here it is not just psychology that is given away, but the psychologist
too. He has emphasised that psychologists' special skills could perhaps
be best exercised in the social services context not by 'acting as
advisors from another profession' but by filling actual social services
roles such as running day or residential establishments. In contrast,
Allen (1979; 1980) worked with the families of mentally handicapped
children as a psychologist in Nottinghamshire Social Services Department, aiming to demystify the psychologist through close integration
with area social workers and other professionals. His post was financed
by deferrment against unfilled social worker establishment. After two
years the county council changed hands and the post was now
regarded as a 'luxury'. When he left, he appears not to have been
replaced.

Observation and Assessment.   A thoughtful exposition of 'classic'
good practice in the social services observation and assessment paradigm
has been presented by the only other psychologist reported here to
have infiltrated a 'real' social services job, in his case as the head of a
community home with education (Hoghughi, 1979a). He has also
produced the first handbook on how to conduct 'observation and

assessment' (Hoghughi, 1980a). A critique of the paradigm has been offered by Sutton (1978b; 1981). The concept of assessment is spreading from child care into other areas of social services practice: some of the risks involved in this for the elderly have been outlined not by a psychologist but by a medical officer (Gray, 1978).

Residential Child Care.   Tutt (e.g. 1974) has addressed wider questions of policy, and Tizard (1977) has examined the relative effects of adoption and life in residential nurseries on the personal and mental development of young children. Foster *et al.* (1977) have described a brief dialogue between psychologists and residential child care staff over the problems of bringing up children in care. Hoghughi (1978) has described his own theoretical and practical approach.

Individual Differences of Children in Care.   Children in community homes with education have provided subjects for a number of studies of individual differences, in running away (Brown *et al.*, 1978), achievement in reading (Matthews, 1975; Sawyer and Brown, 1977; Whittaker, 1977), social background (Ostapiuk *et al.*, 1976) and 'creativity' (Evans and Murray, 1969). Yule and Raynes (1972) related behavioural problems of children in care to separation experiences in care.

Management of Children in Care.   Tutt and Tutt (1975) have examined 150 cases of violence by children or young people, described by professional workers. The majority of these accounts were provided by residential social workers. They concluded *inter alia* that despite social work's heavy emphasis upon 'relationships' social workers as a group appeared to have little understanding of how to contain or cope with violence. They were also shocked in some cases by the observations made, ' . . . shocked because the language of the reports often barely conceals the social worker's aggression towards his client, dubious value judgements fall thick and fast, closely followed by condemnation and abuse'. More recently the behavioural technologies have been offered to the *armamentarium* of the residential social worker (Brown, 1977). The use of a token economy (Brown, 1977; 1978b; Teare and Brown, 1977) and social skills training (see Brown and Sawyer, 1978) in one community home with education have met with the apparent eager co-operation of staff. Gregory and Tweddle (1979) have suggested how residential child care might be improved by teaching independence skills *via* the use of behavioural objectives in children's homes.

Delinquency.   Only Tutt (e.g. 1979) has devoted attention to the wider questions of delinquency outside of the immediate context of residential care.

Social Work.   Despite the enormous importance of social workers to the operation of the social services departments there have been no psychological studies of their work or of psychologists' working with them published in this country. Gregory and Tweddle (1978) have suggested how behavioural objectives might be used to improve one professional activity to which social workers are highly (though not uniquely) prone — meetings. C. Sutton (1979) has written a textbook to relate various bodies of psychological knowledge to social work practice. She has what is probably the unique qualification of all the authors reviewed here of having herself been a local authority social worker before taking up psychology, being therefore aware of both the paucity of social work theory and the real demands of the job. She concludes with an attempt to integrate five psychological models, the psychological, the psychoanalytic/psychodynamic, the social learning/ behavioural, the cognitive and the humanistic, into an 'eclectic approach' for effective casework and counselling. Hoghughi (e.g. 1980b) has presented an extensive critique of social work from one who works inside social services and rejects the conventional disciplinary boundaries. His analysis is empirical and systematic rather than specifically psychological.

Day Care for Young Children.   Some general principles for work in this field were suggested by Sutton and Collins (1977). An independent series of enquiries has been conducted in Tower Hamlets. Coleman *et al.* (1975) have described the establishment of an 'enriched nursery school environment' in one day nursery, whilst Coleman and Laishley (1977; 1978) and Laishley and Coleman (1978) have given a more detailed account of a two-year project in which one of them was attached full-time to work with the six day nurseries within the borough.

Child Abuse.   'Non-accidental injury' has been the central issue, not just of child care, but of the whole life of social services departments throughout the seventies. Especially in the heavily pressed urban authorities it has acted to distort the direction and emphasis of the departments' work. Psychologists have been conspicuously absent from our society's attempts to understand and intervene in this constellation

of problems which, when all else has been taken into consideration, are
quintessentially manifest in behaviours that comprise an aspect of
parent–child interactions. Berger (1975) suggested how factors within
the child might affect the parent–child interaction, and how one might
intervene, but this line of research has not been taken up in this
country. There has been much 'research' into abusive interactions, but
the 'psychological' component of such research has been primarily
psychometric (e.g. Baher, *et al.*, 1976; Smith, *et al.*, 1973). A
behavioural approach to assessment and treatment has been suggested
to social workers (Francis and Sutton, 1976; and in much more detail,
Hutchings, 1980). Reavley and Gilbert (1978) and Hutchings and
Jones (1980) have given examples of behavioural clinical practice in
this field. Where child abuse is suspected in a case it has not as yet
proved possible to mount a controlled trial of alternative innovative
procedures, whatever their theoretical bases. Frude (1980) has collected
a variety of psychological perspectives on child abuse, but though they
shed interesting light upon the problem, and suggest possible departures
for practice, they do not include any actual research in this field by
British psychologists. A retrospective comparative treatment trial,
finding 'developmental day care' far less likely to lead to long-term
institutional care than a residential response to abuse or severe neglect,
has been described by Sutton (1981). Sutton (1980b) has examined
the problem of false–positive identifications on at-risk registers, by
means of Baysian statistics and a hypothetical screening system. An
essential background to any consideration of the wide interpretation
of 'child abuse' is the wide use of physical punishment as part of the
British child-rearing culture, described by Newson and Newson (1968).

The Courts.   King (1976) has drawn attention to the need for the
psychologist involved in social services work that includes the juvenile
court to take account of the social psychological forces at work within
the court itself. Sutton (1978c) has criticised the content of reports to
the juvenile court: he has proposed (1980a) an internal classification
for the knowledge base of expert evidence (from all disciplines), and
means whereby it might be revealed.

Evaluation.   Dunlop (1974) and Cornish and Clarke (1975) evaluated
the outcome of the regimes of what were still called 'approved schools'
at the time of their studies, in terms of reoffending rates. No further
such studies have been made of the 'community homes with education',
and nothing has emerged to suggest that their generally more

'therapeutic' line is more productive than that of their predecessors. A retrospective study of disposals by Leeds juvenile court (Berg *et al.*, 1977) found adjournment a more effective way of ensuring the return to school of non-school-attenders than was supervision by a social worker or probation officer. The retrospective study was followed up by a prospective evaluation (Berg *et al.*, 1978) allotting adjournment or supervision to cases by random number tables (once counter-indicated children had been put aside). The results again favoured adjournment (though less markedly than in the first study). As an unforeseen spin-off the adjournment group also showed a significant advantage in terms of less delinquent behaviour. Berg is not a psychologist: he is a psychiatrist.

Theory.   Despite the psychologisation of many of the human problems that fall under the control of social services departments, there has been little detailed examination of the theoretical and empirical justification for how they are conceived. Much of the detailed critique of popular (and professional) fallacies about 'early experience' by Clarke and Clarke (1976) is relevant to revered and unfounded child care lore. Sutton (1981) has examined the theoretical basis for child care expertise and has found it largely wanting. Other critiques of false psychological theory in social work and in social services departments have come from *outside* of psychology, Rutter (1972) on 'maternal deprivation', Rutter and Madge (1976) on the 'cycle of disadvantage', Morgan (1975) on sub-psychoanalytic child care theories, and (1978) on 'liberal' approaches to juvenile delinquency. Howells (1974) alone reacted to the child abuse panic by looking to theoretical rather than procedural inadequacies as the fundamental flaw in our child welfare system. Rutter and Howells are psychiatrists, Morgan is a sociologist.

Moral Development.   Social work theory and social services practice show an astonishing absence of explicit concern to link children's development to moral values. Psychologists have shared this lack of concern, at least in the published literature. There is as yet no attention to moral development in this context as an object of psychological investigation or intervention in its own right. In the wider world Kohlberg might be fashionable and Makarenko radical, but only Hoghughi (1979b) amongst British psychologists has as yet dared to exercise in print concepts such as 'right and wrong' and 'responsibility'.

Independent Practice. By its very nature psychological investigation or intervention in the work of social services departments has to be at the very least 'by approval' of the local authority, even when conducted under the auspices of an outside agency. Sutton (1977), drawing largely from the US literature, has indicated some of the problems of the psychologist who acts in an independent 'advocate' role. Porteous (1979) has urged the advocacy role on psychologists working *within* the institution of social services: he concluded that 'as an advocate for children and at the same time a counsellor for staff, the psychologist has a distinct role to fulfil'. He did not indicate the contradictory nature of this 'distinct role', nor the personal stress and the conflict that trying to fulfil both requirements within the one institution might involve. Sutton (1980a) has invoked the legal advocate as a means whereby psychology might be brought to the service of the child or family rather than the social services department, 'giving psychology away' in the sense of revealing, betraying or blowing the whistle on bad psychological theory and practice.

In so far as one can tell from the published literature, the decade since the Social Services Act (1970) has seen a minor involvement by psychologists in the affairs of the social services departments, with very slight involvement in the early years when systems and procedures were being first established. The material now published is perhaps sufficient to show certain trends.

1. The largest psychological involvement has been that of educational psychologists. Whatever excellent work might have been achieved by some of these psychologists, it has not yet been made available to the wider community. It should be noted that failure to publish is general to all areas of the work of this branch of psychology (Hart and Taylor, 1979). Educational psychologists' work in observation and assessment centres appears buried within their local systems, perhaps ideologically as much as administratively, and it may be that both for the clients of these systems and for the development of knowledge their efforts are not simply wasted but perhaps even counter-productive.
2. With a very few exceptions the bulk of published material has come from a far smaller body of psychologists, from a whole range of backgrounds. Increasingly, clinical psychologists are contributing in this field, particularly with accounts of practical, empirical research, but it has to be emphasised that many of the psychologists have no 'professional' training in psychology at all. The concerns of social

services departments (and the concerns that they generate) are far wider than encompassed by the present branches of professional psychology, nor do they comprise in themselves a unitary body of knowledge. The suggestion of a single 'child psychology' specialism to cover child care meets problems in this respect. Of the psychologists, some worked *inside* social services departments or in a variety of their various sub-agencies, a couple as social services agents in their own right but the majority as 'psychologists', some being paid by social services direct, some on secondment arrangements. Others worked for outside agencies, AHAs or universities, with various arrangements allowing them to work with social services cases or sub-agencies, others still were wholly 'academic', though dealing with issues central to aspects of social services work. Some were working on research grants to cover specific topics, the majority were contributing to the literature out of their day-to-day practical experience. Very few indeed had an experience stretching back to before the 1970 Act. None of the authors reviewed here was working in Scotland, though it is not clear whether this reflects reality or the present author's parochialism. Within England and Wales the majority were 'provincial': London and the home counties were markedly under-represented.

3. The nature of psychological theory offered varied correspondingly. The psychologies adapted to this new field have included developmental, social, organisational and behavioural. There were a few psychometric studies early on but these seem to have died out, the bulk of publication being related to practicalities. There is a marked dependency upon American models, both theoretical and practical, and some uncritical importation of concepts (e.g. 'community psychology') that do not sit easily in our own social reality. There has not yet emerged any self-conscious body of psychology and psychologists (with the possible exception of the behaviourally oriented) that sees itself as offering a comprehensive psychological response to the problems of social services: the field remains exceedingly fluid.

4. The preponderance of publications (and of course all the work of the educational psychologists) concerns child care issues, presumably reflecting what have become the governing priorities of social services departments. Areas covered include management of children in care (especially community homes), the juvenile court, day care and child abuse. Even within child care, however, there are important omissions: these include the whole question of 'casework' in its

sense of a psychological technique (the very core of most social workers' claim to professionalism), and a host of questions relating to the clients' problems in their natural settings. Outside of child care, with a few exceptions social services activities remain almost wholly untouched. The level at which the psychological work reported here is pitched varies, from grass-roots, minute-by-minute exchanges with clients to wider theoretical and organisational analyses. Implicitly or explicitly the bulk of what has been written has been critical of present social services theory and practice, usually (though not always) at a psychological level rather than at a social, philosophical or political one.

Most of what has been described relates to work conducted very recently, over the last four to five years at most (compare the last review — of child care only — conducted by Gregory, 1977). It is clear that much more psychological work is in the pipeline, and the recent 'initiative' by the SSRC (1980) will doubtless generate more. In total, however, all the psychological work completed, in progress or projected amounts to but a tiny fraction of what could have been done, and when one considers the enormous commitment of social services departments to 'psychological' techniques (wholly untested, and probably mainly invalid) it is an even tinier fraction of what *should* have been done. It must also be admitted that the effects of what has been undertaken to date have probably been minimal at most. Reports of technical advances have little or no effect upon social work training or social services practice (SSRC, 1980), and before psychologists as a body wax pious about this they should recall that their own chief representatives amongst social services departments, the educational psychologists, are themselves unlikely to read the bulk of the materials reported above (see Quicke, 1978). Writers within social work (e.g. C. Sutton, 1979; Sheldon, 1980) who advocate a more informed use of psychology tend to draw more upon American models than upon the growing body of indigenous work.

Psychologists who set out to act as catalysts and change agents for social services should recall the fate of community work which tried to do the same in the early days after the 1970 Act, and ponder on how far (and in what direction) the education service has been affected by the large numbers that work with and within it. They should consider the wider social roles of local government, and the intended functions of its public servants.

The Next Stage?

There are strong suggestions that in our society's long story of dealing
with the poor the zig-zag of history is in the process of another turn.
Once more fundamental, social and economic problems have not been
faced, and continuing economic development has left us with widespread social casualties. Some of our society's powers of provision and
control are now vested in local government social services departments,
and our current emphasis on control is reflected increasingly in the
balance of these departments' activities. The rhetoric of 'help' still
prevails at the formal level, but professionalism in social services
departments has little substance with which to resist the demands of
managerialism and bureaucracy. Much of the effort of social services
departments is devoted to the administration of welfare to the poor,
and the vocabulary and techniques of the various 'helping professions'
involved must be regarded to be in significant part a means towards
regulating their clients' lives, in which the concept of 'needs' has
replaced the concept of sin. If this is to be the way of things for social
services departments in the foreseeable future, then to justify their role
they may seek far better technologies than they have had to date, and
psychology (particularly behavioural psychology) might prove of
increasing interest to them.

Psychology has had its developments too, and has its own minor
crisis to face. Its development has included great advances in applicable
techniques, and the confidence to apply them. The crisis comes from
the joint effects of the increase in numbers and the curtailment of
expansion. The activities and concerns of social services departments,
overlapping as they do with the traditional psychologists' territories of
mental health and education, provide obvious areas for *Lebensraum*.
This is not to imply cynical territorialism as the sole basis for many
psychologists' wishing to involve themselves in social services work.
Most psychologists have a humane and liberal concern for the needy,
and respond readily to the possibility of adapting their own skills to
their aid. Now, however, not only is the spirit willing, there are also
material advantages to doing so, and also perhaps increasing
opportunity.

In seizing such opportunities psychologists should be very careful to
make a certain distinction. They may well be able to do something to
help certain poor people, they may even be able to humanise certain
social services institutions or practices that deal with aspects of poor
peoples' lives. But in doing so they will not be doing anything to affect

the fundamental problem of poverty. This will not be because there are not enough psychologists to help all the poor people or to change all the institutions dealing with them: it is because the underlying problems are economic, social and political. Psychological problems are a manifestation of these problems, they are not their essence. Any success that the psychologist achieves at the psychological level does not change the overall structure, it may rather facilitate it. If employees of social services departments have felt that they were going to change society by 'psychologising' their clients' problems, then their problem was not just one of poor psychology, but of reductionism: providing the departments wtih better psychology will not help the fundamental problems. This is not to deny the possible value and humanity of attention to the psychological problems, either as interim measures or components of a greater whole. Nor should it obscure the fact that there are areas of social services work that are less problematical in this respect, for example aspects of adoption, work with the elderly and the handicapped, and perhaps also the management of day care. And nor, of course, are these considerations which are absent from psychologists' work in mental health or education.

There seems good reason to expect that during the 1980s social services work will be an area of increasing expansion for psychological practice, if for no other reason than much of it falls under the increasingly influential category of Law-and-Order. Given the relatively limited range of goals that psychologists might hope to achieve in this context, what are the most effective and appropriate levels at which their effort might be directed? Should it be towards training? Those psychologists who have glimpsed the 'psychological' component of some social work training have reacted with incredulity: how can such stuff be allowed in universities? What might we do to change this . . . should we not at least expect that psychology is taught by psychologists, or at least be according to a psychologically approved syllabus? Or should more of us become professors of social work? Two psychologists already have, to the horror of the British Association of Social Workers. But then just how effective is professional training anyway in determining subsequent professional behaviour, compared with the powerful forces that will be met in the workplace? Surely it is in the workplace that the psychologist might contribute most . . . but if so, should it be as a psychologist *per se* or as a worker in a real social services job; should it be at a grass-roots level, or in the higher bureaucratic echelons of the local authority, or even in the DHSS itself? And if the goal is to work towards changing the system rather than merely improving on it, is the psychologists' best place outside the system altogether? The 'traditional' outside base is in the universities, 'doing research', but how far is research actually heeded in practice, however relevant it may be? Quite outside of the 'official' system are the community and local action groups, the pressure groups and the political organisations. How far are British psychologists prepared (or able) to follow some of their American colleagues into the courts or on to the political platforms to advocate their clients' needs? The developments within social services over the seventies were quite unforeseeable at the time of heady expectation following the 1970 Act: the possible mutual development of social services departments and psychologists are similarly unforeseeable at the start of the eighties. Last year there was a (probably apocryphal) rumour in circulation that the DHSS was keen to encourage the employment of psychologists within social services departments; social workers, it asserted, were too tainted with lefty sociological ideas . . . psychologists were much more 'responsible' and would provide a countervailing force. Absolute rubbish — or is it? Paradoxically, large numbers of those *social* workers, holding *social* administration degrees with strong *sociological* components, and often holding *socialist* ideals, have worked in *social* services departments in a largely *non-social* manner, directing their efforts in a psychological direction. It can only be hoped that psychologists working in this field adopt a more social world view from the outset.

REHABILITATING OFFENDERS IN THE
COMMUNITY: IMPLICATIONS FOR PENAL
POLICY AND PROFESSIONAL PRACTICE

Eugene B. Ostapiuk and Ian D. Reid*

The first prison I ever saw had inscribed on it, 'Cease to do evil:
learn to do well', but the inscription was on the outside: the
prisoners could not read it.

George Bernard Shaw: *Imprisonment*

Theories of crime are almost as old as the phenomena they seek to
explain. Earliest formulations, for example the writings of Bentham,
did not attempt to provide a theoretical explanation beyond the moral
judgement that when criminals are faced with an opportunity to do
right or wrong they freely choose to do the latter.

In contrast to the classical school of criminology, proponents of the
Positivist School substituted the concept of determinism for free will.
The positivists' view of human behaviour led to explicit theories of
crime, some emphasising social factors, other preferring physical,
psychological or environmental variables to explain scientifically why
certain individuals commit criminal acts. Almost all contemporary
theories of crime are derived from the spirit, if not the concepts, of the
eighteenth-century positivists.

Sociological Formulations

Sociological theories assume many forms, but generally tend to
emphasise external influences which affect large numbers of people.
They highlight the contribution of economic and political changes,
power relationships and the influence of class and status, rather than
the fine grain of individual behavioural experiences.

Such theories are divided into structural and subcultural explanations (S. Reid, 1976). Most structural theories (e.g. Cloward and Ohlin,
1960; Cohen, 1955) suggest that, despite a basic equality of personal

*Authorship should be considered equal. The contents of this chapter represent
the authors' views alone and in no way commit the DHSS, the Home Office or
the Department of Employment.

interests and abilities, certain groups suffer a fundamental inequality of opportunity to actualise these talents in socially legitimate ways. The discrepancy between aspiration and the means of attainment is offered as a sufficient criminogenic condition. The subcultural approach (e.g. Mays, 1963) asserts that subcultures with high rates of offending socialise their individual members according to standards that are deviant from middle-class norms; further, that as not all families in the subculture are offenders, not all boys will become delinquent. Although the subcultural view strongly emphasises the role of learning, it has limitations; specifically, it is confined to socially disadvantaged settings, and says nothing about the acquisition of criminal behaviours by those in more advantaged subcultures.

Biological Formulations

The enduring belief that delinquents are biologically or genetically inferior to the 'general population' persists, although there is limited evidence to support such a conclusion. Most theories search for types of people who are uniquely disposed to criminal behaviour because of certain genetic deficiencies, physiological excesses or constitutional deficits.

The notion that criminals are recognised by physical features was postulated in the nineteenth century by Lombroso (see Lombroso, 1911). He claimed that many criminals physically resembled animals lower in the evolutionary scale than man. More recently, Sheldon (1942) proposed a link between body build and personality. Several studies have found an association between broad and muscular body build and crime, but most are marred by serious defects in experimental design (e.g. Gibbons, 1963). A much better study by Glueck and Glueck (1956) compared 500 chronic delinquents matched on a host of demographic variables with 500 non-delinquents. They claimed that significantly more delinquents were predominantly mesomorphic than non-delinquents. A substantial proportion of delinquents, however, were not mesomorphic. The Gluecks concluded 'it is quite apparent that physique alone does not adequately explain delinquent behaviour, it is none the less clear that, in conjunction with other forces, it does bear a relationship to delinquency'.

Following an initial report in 1961, several studies reported a biological basis for the 'aggressive psychopath' — the extra Y-chromosome. Jarvik *et al.* (1973) concluded that as criminals are the only population in which the extra Y-chromosome occurs significantly more often than the extra X-chromosome 'an extra Y-chromosome predisposes to aggressive behaviour'. Unfortunately for this position, it is still the case that most violent crimes are committed by chromosomally normal people and that the majority of XYY-males are neither criminal nor prone to aggressiveness that they are unable to control.

The genetic contribution to criminal behaviour has been extensively studied using a variety of experimental methods including family, twin and adoption studies. Reviewing these Feldman (1977) judiciously concluded 'Biological influences are less important than their extreme proponents would urge but of greater importance than those wedded to a solely learning account would allow'. Nietzel (1979) has been less restrained, asserting that:

> The present data indicate that genetics play a very small part in determining criminal behaviour. Although some data suggest only a possible genetic potential for a very select range of criminal behaviour . . . it is simply unreasonable to assume that there is a direct link between genetics and the enormous array of legally deviant behaviour which the criminologist seeks to explain.

Psychological Formulations

Psychoanalytic theories of crime continue to be the dominant orientation of many mental health professionals who seek to explain and treat criminal behaviour. The underlying assumption is that criminal behaviour is a manifestation of some form of personality disturbance in which internal controls are unable to control the aggressive and antisocial instincts of the id. Theoretical speculations are legion, including the need to be punished (Glover, 1960), failure to be governed by the reality principle, and a means of obtaining compensatory gratification of basic needs such as love (Alexander and Healy, 1935).

Criticisms of the psychoanalytic view are well documented elsewhere (e.g. Feldman, 1977). Suffice it to say here that many writers feel that it contains numerous logic-of-science errors and lacks empirical verification. Moreover, such interpretations of crime are vastly discrepant from patterns of actual criminal behaviour. Freud's assertion that criminals seek to be caught (Freud, 1961), is amply refuted by the extremes to which criminals will go to avoid detection. Evidence suggests that they do this most successfully, and view their success as gratifying, not frustrating or guilt-inducing as the theory would suggest. Finally, psychoanalytic theories fail to explain why many forms of criminal behaviour are planned and well organised, rather than compulsive and irrational.

Eysenck's view of personality development asserts that while previous learning experience and current situational stimuli are both important, in the long term largely inherited predispositions play a major role (Eysenck and Eysenck, 1969). His approach, an example of the consistency model of personality, would expect the same persons to behave rather consistently in different places and at different times. In contrast, the specificity model of individual differences emphasises the extent to which learning experiences and current situational stimuli interact to produce differences between individuals, i.e. the specificity model attributes individual differences in behaviour to external events and not 'personality'. Many behaviourally orientated theorists would object to the Eysenckian position on the grounds that moral behaviour is specific to the situation in which it is expected to occur. Thus, Mischel (1976) has concluded 'the data on self-control and moral behaviour do not support the existence of a unitary, intrapsychic moral agency like the super ego, nor do they suggest a unitary trait of conscience or honesty'.

Feldman (1977) has sought a compromise in the consistency *versus* specificity debate. He suggested that both camps tend to assume that a given degree of consistency in a particular population means that all individuals in the population contribute to it equally. A plausible alternative view is that some people are more consistent than others. Experimental support is provided by Olweus (1975):

> Eysenckian personality dimensions are likely to make a useful contribution to the explanation of criminal behaviour, but more to its acquisition than its performance or maintainence, and much more in the case of extreme, than in the case of median scores. Even in acquisition, by extreme scorers, personality will only be part of the story; situational variables will play a significant role. (Feldman, 1977)

There are a variety of other psychological theories of criminal behaviour, including Piaget's (1932) theory of moral development, Jeffery's (1965) proposition that criminal behaviour is acquired according to the principles of operant conditioning and Bandura's (1969) social learning formulations. According to Nietzel (1979), however, Feldman's formulation 'represents one of the most comprehensive sociopsychological accounts of crime currently available. Feldman's theory is relevant to crimes against both persons and property'. Nietzel applauded Feldman's willingness to confront the social realities of crime in a more satisfactory way than does a theory based solely on learning principles. The inclusion of personality predispositions acknowledges a differential susceptibility to acquire a repertoire favourable to offending, and his analysis of labelling theory amply illustrates its potentially harmful effects. Perhaps Feldman's major achievement is that not only does his integrated learning theory provide an excellent framework from which to investigate personality predispositions, learning and social labelling, but it also gives a clear lead for practical innovations in crime control and correction. It is unfortunate that many traditional approaches (both penal and psychological) are not based on such a sound theoretical basis.

Treatment Interventions

Traditional Penal Methods

The variety of methods conventionally used by the penal system includes probation, fining and various types and time periods of institutional confinement. Unfortunately these methods have developed empirically and are not based to any great extent on the findings of sociological or psychological research. Indeed in some instances, particularly in the case of certain forms of imprisonment, it is difficult to see any clear rationale behind a particular provision. Many institutional programmes have hopelessly confused goals, usually involving potentially contradictory aims, i.e. punishment, rehabilitation and deterrence. To further complicate the situation, any manifestation of punishment, rehabilitation, etc. are always subject to the political expedients of central government. It is therefore not surprising that conclusions as to the efficacy of traditional penal methods are typically modest at best, and sometimes frankly pessimistic, as in the case of the following quotation by Schur (1965):

> No research has been done to date which enables us to say that one treatment programme is better than another or that enables us to examine a man and specify the treatment he needs. There is no evidence that probation is better than institutions, that institutions are better than probations . . . [so] much of what is now being done about crime may be so wrong that the net effect of that action may be to increase rather than decrease crime . . . none of the researches conducted to date answers these questions.

Psychotherapeutic Methods

The most ambitious attempt is still the earliest reported, namely the
Cambridge-Somerville Youth Study carried out between 1937 and
1945 (Teuber and Powers, 1953). Several hundred pre-adolescent
American boys judged likely to become offenders, were matched in
pairs for a number of variables expected to be relevant, and were then
randomly assigned to counsellors free to adopt a psychoanalytic or
client-centred (Rogerian) approach, or to a no-treatment control group.
At follow-up the groups were virtually identical on several official
indices of offending. This disappointing result has been repeated several
times with convicted offenders. Grant and Grant (1959) assessed 'level
of maturity' in three groups of 20 military offenders, which were of
respectively high, low and mixed level of maturity. Each group under-
went group psychotherapy for a nine-week period, but although the
high-maturity group are said to have responded significantly better
overall on the criterion of return to military duty, the Grants' own
conclusion was 'No significant differences were found which could be
attributed to supervisors' predicted effectiveness'.

Warren *et al.* (1966) compared intensive treatment in the community
of a group of boys classified into eight sub-groups by two levels of
maturity (high and low), and four types of personality (neurotic, non-
neurotic, etc.) with a similar group of boys undergoing equally intensive
treatment in an institution. On the basis of a 15-month follow-up,
results suggested a more favourable outcome for the community-treated
neurotics as compared to their institutionally-treated counterparts.
Only trends were observed for the other sub-groups. Hood and Sparks
(1970), however, cited several cogent criticisms of the study, perhaps
the most significant being that treatment programmes were constantly
modified over the course of the project, so that even if any difference
in outcome occurred it would be very difficult to identify the active
elements of the treatment programme which were responsible. A
British study by Cornish and Clarke (1975) also produced disappointing
results. They compared, over a ten-year period, the effects of two
regimes at the Kingswood Training School. One regime was of
traditional type, formal and highly structured, while the other was a
'therapeutic community' involving twice-daily discussion groups. Both
methods resulted in a 70 per cent reconviction rate.

Criticisms of psychotherapeutic interventions are detailed elsewhere
(Logan, 1972; Feldman, 1977). No typology of offenders nor treatment
has been shown to be reliable or valid. Further, there is the even more
fundamental consideration that there exists clear evidence (Rachman,

1972) of the lack of success of any psychotherapeutic approach over and above spontaneous recovery. If the psychotherapies fail to help those who suffer from personal difficulties and seek help, it follows that attempting to change the behaviour of those who do not seek help and who indeed benefit from their behaviour, will be even more difficult. To date, psychotherapeutic methods have failed to demonstrate that they are able to meet this challenge.

A History of Failure

There may be several important reasons why classical treatment approaches to the delinquency problem have had such limited success, and it is worth considering some of these, in the light of empirical evidence. First, while some offenders may be deterred from re-offending, others may become more likely to re-offend following penal treatment (Feldman, 1977). Indeed Stumphauzer (1970, 1973) has shown that offenders in institutions may encourage further offending by providing inmates with new deviant skills and ample reinforcement for their use. Secondly, traditional penal institutions are highly artificial environments mostly isolated from the community, hence less likely to prepare individuals for the stresses of the real world. More times than not an individual is trained to fit neatly into the institution rather than his local community and neighbourhood (Hersen, 1976). Thirdly, there is plenty of evidence to suggest that skills taught in a highly artificial environment are exceedingly difficult to transfer to the real world (Repucci and Saunders, 1974). Finally, traditional approaches to offender rehabilitation have paid all too little attention to adequate evaluation of both their own treatment efficacy and comparative cost-effectiveness with alternative procedures (Logan, 1972; Bailey, 1966).

Behavioural Methods

In the last ten to fifteen years a new trend in offender care and rehabilitation has come to play an increasingly important role. The behaviour modification approach has drawn widespread interest both from practitioners (as evidenced by the volume of published papers, books and journal articles), the lay public and the media. There is by now a well-documented body of literature detailing promising results of behavioural methods in offender rehabilitation (Davidson and Seidman, 1974; Braukmann and Fixsen, 1975; Feldman, 1977; Johnson, 1977; Stumphauzer, 1973). At the same time, this new approach has not been without its critics, ranging from those who have questioned its application to offender care (Burgess, 1965; Sage, 1974),

through those who suggest it is open to abuse by institutional staff or
the system (Trotter, 1975; Mitford, 1973), to those who consider the
application of behavioural techniques as unconstitutional or an
infringement of civil liberties (Trotter, 1974; Start, 1974).

Most of the new developments have occurred overseas, largely in the
United States. A wide range of behavioural principles have been put to
use in effecting behaviour change with delinquents. Positive reinforcement, social modelling and behavioural rehearsal, token economies,
level systems, response cost, aversion techniques, negative reinforcement, time out, are by no means an exhaustive list of procedures
implemented in predominantly institution-based programmes, such as
the Carl Holton School for boys (Jesness, 1974) and Draper Prison
(Milan *et al.*, 1974), the controversial START programme (Start,
1974), and community-based programmes such as those at Achievement
Place (Phillips, 1968) and other similar 'teaching parent' family homes.
Completing the spectrum is the work of researchers like Schwitzgebel
(1964) and his 'street corner' programmes, and Fo and O'Donnell
(1975) and their 'buddy system' project.

It seems that the American imagination, always restless, continues
to generate new programmes for handling the juvenile offender. Walk-
in 'day centres' for juvenile delinquents run by the Probation
Department of New York as alternatives to detention, the innovative
use of such methods as restitution, weekend incarceration, halfway
houses, deferred prosecution, work and education release and
residential support services are a few examples of new strategies being
pursued in preference to institutional programmes (Nelson *et al.*,
1979). The Colorado 'New Pride' project (Project New Pride, 1978)
perhaps typifies the multi-component programme approach to the
delinquency problem. It has demonstrated that the serious juvenile
offender who has not succeeded in traditional programmes can be
rehabilitated in the community without risk. Emphasis on individual
treatment undertaken in the offender's own environment is claimed to
be the biggest reason for the programme's success. The 'New Pride'
project focuses on court-supervised youths aged 14 to 17. It stresses
diagnostic and behavioural assessments with a view to remedial
education, job preparation and placement, and follow-up services and
guidance. A feature of this project is the co-operation between federal
government and private non-profit-making agencies with a view to
developing a strategy to support the project after federal funding ceases.
Because the project has been so successful, as shown by a very low
recidivism rate and very favourable cost-effectiveness figures, federal

funding to the tune of millions of dollars is being made available for a
national replication of the programme. With such a growth of non-
institutional projects for offender rehabilitation in the United States it
is perhaps not surprising that the total number of residents in juvenile
detention facilities has been steadily declining throughout the 1970s.
The rise in the total number of open facilities is consistent with stated
goals of diverting juveniles from institutions altogether, or of placing
them in small community-based residences near their homes (US
Bureau of the Census, 1979).

In the Light of Experience

There remains a number of well-founded and justified criticisms even
of the best behavioural programmes. In most cases the efficacy of the
techniques used has been demonstrated in small-scale projects within
existing institutional programmes. In these cases, practitioners have
been preoccupied with proving the usefulness of their behavioural
technology and their ability to change specific behaviours, rather than
with changing the overall framework of rehabilitation. Secondly, the
failure of behavioural practitioners to evaluate separately the effects of
existing traditional penal strategies has significant implications for the
reliability of the behavioural change resulting from behavioural
procedures, in that the former may be compounding the effects of the
latter (Johnson, 1977). Perhaps the most significant criticism levelled
at behavioural programmes is their failure, with a few exceptions
(Wetzel, 1966; Fodor, 1972; Wolfe and Marino, 1975), to address
themselves to the actual offence behaviours of their client population.
In an excellent review of this area, Emery and Marholin (1977) have
recently criticised the irrelevancy of the behaviours often targeted for
behaviour intervention. Other reviewers have pointed out that illegal
acts *per se* have seldom been considered the target of behavioural
intervention (Johnson, 1977; Feldman, 1977), with the possible
exception of sexual offenders where there exists a fairly well-established
assessment and treatment technology. Finally, the behaviour modification programmes undertaken in institutions are equally susceptible
to generalisation problems. Nevertheless, the behavioural approach has
at least brought with it an emphasis on informed innovation and the
goals of prevention as well as rehabilitative behaviour change.

Developments in the UK

The winds of change have been very slow to blow in the UK, and where
change has occurred it has been a question of reorganising resources

rather than trying out new treatment approaches. The application of behavioural methods to treatment of offenders in the UK has been sporadic and piecemeal, with little co-ordination of effort and even less dissemination of information concerning techniques and resources used. Whenever attempts have been made it has invariably been the case that the behavioural programmes have been merely a small component within the parameters of a traditional system. The token economy based house-unit programme at Franklin House (Aycliffe School) is one such example (Hoghughi *et al.*, 1977). Examples of a comprehensive behavioural programme spanning the entire treatment regime of an institution are difficult to find. Only one such case is known to the authors — that of Glenthorne Youth Treatment Centre, a DHSS establishment dealing with seriously disturbed, dangerous and delinquent children up to the age of 18 (Reid and Ostapiuk, 1979). When one considers non-institutional, community-based schemes offering rehabilitative support to young offenders the picture seems little better. A recent report by the Manpower Services Commission (1979) listed 28 projects offering a range of support systems under the broad heading of rehabilitation, for offenders, ex-offenders, and those considered 'at risk'. Most, if not all, of these projects seem to concentrate on tackling the core problem of offender behaviour by concentrating on teaching work skills and habits, and providing accommodation. Only five of the schemes are offered as alternatives to custodial detention. The basic premiss seems to be that a substantial proportion of those young people who become customers of the criminal justice system face multiple personal and practical problems amongst which unemployment features significantly. Clearly, offender unemployment is in part a consequence of an individual's offending; equally it is often a contributory factor to continued offending. This interrelationship, together with a lack of basic educational and self-help skills, and the fact that unemployed offenders tend to be disproportionately located in depressed, decaying, inner-city areas, suggests that the solution to offender difficulties cannot be developed in isolation. Supported work programmes can be an important step towards increasing confidence and motivation to survive in the real world. What additionally is needed is a combined provision on a broad front with inputs from a variety of sources.

What follows is a description of a new project in the UK concerned with offender rehabilitation in the community, which strives to bring together into a systematic, controlled programme some of the requirements discussed above.

The Shape Project

Background

The origins of the current Shape project go back to 1973, when Shape Housing Association, primarily concerned with the temporary renovation of 'short-life' properties in the inner-city area of Birmingham, established a hostel for unemployed ex-offenders and individuals 'at risk' who comprised part of their workforce. This hostel was shortly afterwards recognised by the Home Office as part of their after-care hostel scheme. At this stage no formal intervention programme was laid down; the aim was simply to bring together two desperate needs to the advantage of both, namely to provide unemployed juvenile offenders with an opportunity for work by renovating desperately needed housing accommodation for low-income families. By 1977 a planned rehabilitation programme was introduced to the hostel project, which was by then directly supervised by the Shape Trust independently of the Housing Association. The goal of the newly constituted project was to be the provision of living accommodation, work and work-skills training, and social, or rather 'survival' skills training for adolescent and young adult offenders and disadvantaged 'at risk' youths, in conditions closely approximating those of the local community from which clients had come and to which they were likely to return. From its inception the new programme was supervised by clinical psychologists with experience of behavioural programmes with young offenders. The kind of training and support offered was to be deliberately practical, down to earth, and related to the client's survival in his own community, independent of statutory agency input. A more detailed description of the early developments of the project and the thinking behind the treatment components may be found elsewhere (Ostapiuk and Reid, in press; Reid, Feldman and Ostapiuk, 1980). The Shape 'survival skills' programme can be separated into three distinct phrases:

Stage 1   behavioural assessment and target setting;
Stage 2   implementation of individual programmes;
Stage 3   survival in the community.

Stage One

The main hostel base of the project (including accommodation for a warden and residents, and the administrative office) is situated in a terrace of houses in a run-down inner-city area of Birmingham. The hostel can accommodate a maximum of six residents, two residents to a bedroom; other facilities which are shared include a kitchen, bathroom and lounge. The property is sub-standard, short-life and in very poor state of repair.

The Programme.   Stage One is the induction and assessment phase of a resident's stay at Shape. The minimum period that a client stays in the Stage 1 hostel is four to five weeks, although some individuals may stay considerably longer, either to complete assessment, or in order to learn basic self-help and personal hygiene skills which are considered prerequisites for the next stage of the programme.

Hostel Manager Scheme.   The hostel manager is elected by his peers, where feasible; otherwise he is appointed by staff. He will normally be a client in the last week or so of this stay in Stage 1, and is appointed for a period of one week. The manager is responsible for the supervision, upkeep, cleaning and smooth running of the hostel, he is the clients' spokesman in representations to staff. He does not necessarily have any specific cleaning or other duties, except where lack of numbers means that there are jobs not covered. His example, by modelling appropriate behaviours, is important to new residents and affords staff the opportunity to assess his ability to take on greater responsibility. He earns more credits than other residents.

Hostel Upkeep Scheme.   Each client moving into the Stage 1 hostel is given a particular area as well as his own bedroom to clean. Areas of the hostel that require constant upkeep are rotated among residents on a weekly basis. Clients volunteer for a job area which is then checked daily. If, having failed to maintain his given area to an agreed level, the client has been prompted and still fails to comply, he forfeits his credit earnings.

Work Experience Scheme.   The programmed week for Stage 1 residents is divided into two parts, hostel activity days and normal work days. On hostel activity days, Monday and Friday, residents can participate in organised leisure pursuits, hostel meetings, major hostel clean-ups, or they can visit probation officers, social workers, etc. On normal work days — Tuesday, Wednesday and Thursday — residents are expected to follow a standard work routine, which is kept as close as possible to that found in any normal works environment. They are checked for being up on time and ready for work in the morning. While at work they are observed and checked for following supervisor's instructions, meeting set targets, and appropriate social behaviour in a work setting. These categories are monitored carefully every day throughout the week, as compliance means credit earnings which are converted to pocket money on 'pay-day' – Friday. While in Stage 1 residents remain unemployed and so have to 'sign on' on Fridays, to draw unemployment and/or supplementary benefits which are then topped up by expenses earned from the daily workforce scheme. Work projects undertaken in Stage 1 range from contractual renovation of short-life property to voluntary, neighbourhood clean-up jobs.

Self Government System. Throughout their stay in Stage 1 of the programme all residents are encouraged to participate fully in decision-making processes where these concern day-to-day running of the hostel, hostel rules, imposing sanctions against non-compliant residents, etc. Thus each resident contributes to the checks and balances needed for the smooth running of the project. Hostel meetings, whether called by residents through the hostel manager, or by staff, are also useful as teaching sessions where appropriate socially acceptable verbal behaviours can be modelled by staff, rehearsed by clients and then reinforced both by staff and other residents.

Credit Systems. While unemployed in Stage 1, residents can make up their statutory income by expenses calculated from credits accumulated during the week. These credits are akin to points awarded for a variety of set targets which are clearly stated and explained to each new client, including each target's tariff value. Credits can be earned from the hostel manager, hostel upkeep, and the work experience schemes described above; they are checked off daily on the Hostel Management Checksheet to which the client has constant access, so that he can see his progress day to day. Every time credits are awarded or stopped the reasons for doing so are clearly explained to the client in order to provide additional social reinforcement or the opportunity for learning alternative, appropriate responses.

Assessment. In addition to weekly monitoring of a credit earnings, which provides a guide to a client's improvement in specific task-related behaviours, several other assessment measures are used which relate to general social behaviour and specific social or survival skills. These measures, which include the *Shape Behaviour Rating Scale*, the

Self-reported Offence Questionnaire and the *Personal Data Record* (Ostapiuk, 1977), form the basis of individual client assessments following completion of Stage 1. Staff observations and ratings are made available to each client during the assessment meeting, when specific problem areas are agreed upon and targeted for the next stage of the programme.

Behavioural Contract.   The whole assessment process is concluded by a written behavioural contract which represents an agreement between the client and staff on how the client is to proceed to the next phase of the programme. It is made clear that this contract has no legal force; it simply represents a clear statement of targets that the client will work towards, the consequences of achieving such targets, and the obligations of staff towards the client in return for improvements in his behaviour. The behavioural contract will be reviewed periodically, and changed by mutual agreement if necessary. It is signed by client and staff.

Stage Two

Having successfully completed the assessment period and agreed upon a behavioural contract, the client moves to Stage 2 of the programme. This is the period of wider skills training. Clients are accommodated in smaller house units, usually terraced houses, where each resident has his own private room/bedsit, and shares other house facilities with a maximum of two or three other residents. Each client is expected to cook for himself, look after his room and belongings, pay rent weekly, and live amicably with the other residents. Stage 2 properties are of a much higher standard than the induction hostel, although they remain short-life units.

The Programme.   Over and above the behavioural contract based on the formal assessment of individual clients, there are a number of prerequisite behaviours which must be present at strength before considering a resident's move to the less supervised semi-independent status of Stage 2. These include: (a) hygiene/personal appearance; (b) upkeep of personal rooms and belongings; (c) payment of rent; (d) handling money/budgeting expenses for week; (e) shopping; (f) simple cooking; (g) time-keeping/regular work habits. Although any of these may be targeted in the behavioural contract for closer attention and specific help, they must occur frequently enough, or be of sufficient strength in a client's behavioural repertoire, not to jeopardise his chance of success in Stage 2.

Work.   Those clients who are ready for full-time employment, in terms of the criteria used in the work experience scheme of Stage 1, and whose assessment has indicated sufficient motivation and interest in work, are encouraged and helped to find a job. Clients not yet ready to take up full-time employment for whatever reason are channelled back into the Stage 1 work experience scheme.

Skills Training.   Individual target behaviours specified in a client's behavioural contract will often necessitate specific skills training sessions, whether on an individual or group basis.

(A) Individual target behaviours such as managing expenses and earnings appropriately, assertive response training, interpersonal conflict resolution, etc. are typically tackled on a one-to-one basis. Modelling by staff of acceptable verbal and physical behaviours, and rehearsal by client of modelled responses, usually occurs in role-played situations, where feedback on a client's performance can be given immediately either by staff or peers.

(B) Group programmes usually take two forms. (i) Problem-solving sessions, where specific issues are raised and discussed, and solutions offered by group members. The emphasis is placed on exploring short- and long-term consequences of particular behaviours or courses of action. Both staff and clients provide social reinforcement for appropriate coping responses, and alternatives, equally acceptable responses, are rehearsed and learned. (ii) Group training sessions, e.g. job interview skills training sessions where all clients where possible participate in the same structured programme of skills teaching. Video equipment and specialised assessment procedures are used in these sessions in order to demonstrate the effectiveness of particular training procedures.

Assessment.   The progress of all clients in Stage 2, whether employed full-time or on the work experience scheme, is regularly monitored. For those who remain with the Shape programme the credit earnings scheme provides information of daily target behaviours. The *Shape Behaviour Rating Scale* is a regular assessment measure; it remains the formal instrument for evaluating client progress throughout the Shape programme. In addition to Shape-based measures, emphasis is given to independent assessments of clients made by their referring agency, whether probation or social services. This means that probation officers and social workers are encouraged where feasible to contribute their evaluations of clients from the standpoint of non-involved, independent observers. Where progress breaks down a client may move back to Stage 1 or be re-targeted in his contract.

Stage Three

This represents the generalisation of the Shape programme. Clients who
have successfully achieved targets stipulated in their behavioural
contracts and who have settled down in full-time employment are
moved on to fully independent accommodation – a flat of their own.
Here it is possible to observe whether newly learned skills stand the
test of time in the real world. Each client is now fully responsible for
managing his own affairs; he pays rent to a landlord, usually a housing
association, and is linked to the Shape programme only by agreement.
The Shape Trust still remains the 'home base', a resource centre of
information and practical help in case of difficulties. In return, the
Trust encourages a 'graduate' to feed back his experiences and offer
help and advice to new entrants into the programme. Successful clients
are powerful models to residents in the project and their influence is
thus capitalised upon.

Follow-up.   Every effort is made to keep in touch with clients once
they 'graduate' from the programme. Probation officer and social
workers are important in providing constant feedback on individual
clients, whether they remain in a job, and, most importantly, whether
they keep out of trouble with the law. In this respect the *Self-reported
Offence Questionnaire* is designed primarily as a follow-up measure.

Implications for Future Developments

Cost-effectiveness

In recent years there has been an increasing interest in the cost of
treatment, particularly in the USA. In the present worsening economic
climate consideration of the cost-effectiveness of treatment programmes
is unavoidable. In the UK this move represents a considerable departure
from traditional practice. There are several good reasons for including
a monetary criterion in the evaluation of treatment methods (Adams,
1967). It is clear that not all offenders are suited to or benefit from
detention, therefore certain penal provisions may well be needlessly
inefficient and a waste of scarce resources. Moreover certain offenders
may actually be harmed by the penal process. In addition to being
presented with an opportunity to learn new delinquent skills, the
offender's economic status and potential are reduced and his family
and the community are indirectly punished, since the offender neither

contributes to the economy of the state as a worker and taxpayer, nor to the family as a wage-earner. As an inmate he becomes instead the object of state spending and his family the recipient of state aid. Furthermore, comparison of relative costs would allow valid choices between programmes where perhaps there are insignificant differences in treatment outcome.

A monetary yardstick is powerful and versatile. It speaks the language of the policy-maker and budget-keeper, and for precisely this reason cost-effectiveness will become an increasingly important consideration in future interventions with delinquents. It is to be hoped that there will be a move away from the traditional means of allocating resources based on current fashion (e.g. intermediate treatment) or political popularity (e.g. the 'short-sharp-shock' approaches). Although both of these 'treatments' are widely different in terms of underlying ideology, both suffer a common lack of any coherent treatment technology. Intermediate treatment has several laudable aims including the teaching of educational skills, the reduction of stigmatisation, etc., which it is assumed will reduce delinquency, while the short-sharp-shock view suggests that punishment will reduce violent behaviour. Little concerted attempt is made by the proponents of either approach to specify the treatment methods to be used, how they will be evaluated, the outcome measures to be used and the types of training that staff will need to implement treatment programmes. In future, perhaps the distributors of resources will demand that members of the helping professions will establish their treatment attempts on a scientific basis. Logan (1972) evaluated the scientific acceptability of outcome studies of corrective efficacy on the basis of ten criteria, and Feldman (1977) has added two more. Perhaps future allocation of resources to corrective programmes should be contingent on how well they meet these twelve criteria proposed by Logan and Feldman.

If this were to become the convention, it would have considerable implications for the location of treatment programmes. Present penal institutions with their methods derived largely from trial and error, lack of attention to sociological and psychological research findings and conflicting goals would seem particularly ill-suited to the adoption of a scientific approach. It may well be that smaller, more coherent units such as the Shape Project described above, are better able to adopt a scientific approach.

Utilisation of Resources

The largest single problem facing voluntary projects is how to implement a treatment programme using the limited resources available. In our experience, the ingenious use of scarce resources requires just as much time and attention as the development of the therapeutic programme itself.

Funding a voluntary project is not easy. The 'vicious circle' effect is most obvious when starting a project. Money is needed to prove a scheme effective, but agencies are cautious and prefer to fund those programmes which have already demonstrated some degree of efficacy! This is not to say that funding is impossible to obtain. The Home Office and DHSS may provide grant support for the therapeutic aspects of a programme and essential, related needs. Additional finance may be available from other government departments, for example urban-aid money from the Department of Employment, and funding through Manpower Services Commission can be used to employ workforce staff and finance property renovation. Housing is a constant problem for many voluntary projects. They are obliged to compete with other agencies and private individuals, but are in a relatively weak position because of limited finance. More often than not the provision of hostels depends on the availability of short-life properties, most of which are in a state of disrepair. Thus further scarce resources must be used to renovate and maintain the basic facilities provided by short-life properties.

Limited resources make maximum use of existing community resources imperative. Facilities vary from area to area, but several examples from the Shape Project highlight the kinds of resource which can be utilised. It has been possible to establish links with the local Job Centre personnel dealing with those unemployed persons who have histories of offending. Because of these links it has been possible to develop a system of referring Shape clients for job-seeking interviews at the Centre. Job Centre staff are agreeable to participate in the evaluation of client effectiveness in interviews and to standardise feedback from potential employers on the interview performance of Shape clients.

The project has also been fortunate enough to develop fruitful links with the local police. In addition to the formal liaison between the police and Shape clients, members of the police are also involved in a range of activities within the project. They have been involved in skills training programmes and in the evaluation of clients' behaviour change and they have voluntarily offered additional supervision for leisure pursuits and on project holidays. The benefits of the formal and informal links with the police cannot be over-estimated.

Finally, links with the Physical Education Department of Birmingham University have proved very valuable. It has been possible to enlist the help of the physical education and sports centre staff to devise a leisure/recreation programme for the Shape clients. Access to sporting facilities provides a potent source of reinforcement for our clients as well as an opportunity to observe and assess clients' behaviour in an environment very different from the hostel setting. Moreover, sporting and social interactions with university students allow our clients to observe successful behaviour and to practice the skills themselves. Both clients and university staff report that the formal contacts have been mutually satisfying.

Consideration for Future Planning

The increasing body of evaluative data on behavioural programmes with offenders combines with our own practical experiences to highlight several issues which merit very serious consideration.

Despite increasing discussion in the psychological literature of ethical questions, few programmes seem overtly concerned with such challenges. Perhaps the guidelines provided by Ayllon (1975) are a useful basis for the development of future programmes. His suggestions included voluntary participation, individualised treatment and the right to discontinue treatment at any time. Nietzel (1979) has suggested that 'a much needed "ethical" contribution from the professionals would be a behavioural analysis of the means by which the public can increase its inputs into discussions of values, ethics and policy as they relate to offender rehabilitation'. With regard to community programmes it is suggested that maximum community/client input be encouraged in order to yield the most meaningful outcome, that the local population should be actively involved in the development of programmes and that citizen-professional review boards should be established for local programmes. Existing programmes could benefit from the incorporation of such suggestions.

The innovations recommended for inclusion in the treatment of delinquency have grave implications for present professional training. Even a cursory glance at many professional training courses, including those of clinical psychologists, psychiatric registrars, social workers and to some extent probation officers, show that relatively little attempt is made:

(a) to identify the *actual* skills needed to design and implement therapeutic programmes (for example, are the members of the

helping professions *actually* socially skilled and able to model these
behaviours?);
(b) to train such skills formally and evaluate trainees' proficiency in
    them as an integral part of their professional qualification.

Far too much emphasis is still placed on the 'academic excellence' of
students' performance. As Burgess (1979) has so rightly pointed out,
the pursuit of academic excellence may be a justifiable goal for certain
academic occupations. We would argue that this preoccupation is far
less justified, indeed in some instances is positively harmful to the
development of the 'helpful professions'. A professional qualification
in clinical psychology may imply to other professions some level of
expertise or competence in a wide range of areas, but at present there
is no additional structured training available in the UK to equip
psychologists to deal with the ever developing number of roles in the
community they are expected to fill (Tully *et al.*, 1978). In contrast,
both undergraduate teaching and postgraduate training in community
psychology are being offered by a growing number of universities and
colleges in the United States, where increasing sensitivity over urgent
social problems has led to a greater willingness to question the appropriateness of existing roles for applied psychologists and to experiment
with new ones (Orford, 1979). If, as many hope, we are to be seen as
experts and therefore worthy of an increased sphere of influence, close
attention needs to be paid to the origin and development of post-
qualification training. If not at the professional clinical level, where
will the professional skills be formally taught and evaluated? This seems
one of the most serious problems threatening any possible increase in
the influence of psychologists in the field of behaviour modification
with delinquents. Our anxiety in this respect is further compounded
by the fear that the 'trainers' (including ourselves), by virtue of their
own selection, have not necessarily demonstrated nor updated the
skills needed to design, implement and manage complex programmes.
If this is the case, how must the trainers change, and who should train
them? We would hope that the same positive planning be applied to
these issues as is traditionally applied to an individual client's problems.

Concluding Comment

We hope to have illustrated some of the past and present approaches to
delinquency and their generally unimpressive results. This is not
intended as a criticism of the personnel involved, but as an indictment
of systems which require enthusiastic and idealistic staff to operate

ill-considered or even harmful programmes. There are no easy answers. There are nevertheless a number of highly promising theoretical and practical developments. Research advances in psychology and sociology clearly show that institutional treatment for delinquents is at best ineffective and expensive, and at worst harmful and expensive. If our primary aim is to modify behaviour there is a need for provisions to reflect the problem behaviours under scrutiny and the resources available to deal with them. The case for an increase in community facilities based on scientific principles and using objective methods is very strong indeed.

The growing awareness of the need for cost-effectiveness and the desirability of incorporating a monetary criterion when evaluating treatments are to be welcomed. These steps towards objectivity and improved efficacy draw attention to the fact that present training courses fail to provide members of the helping professions with the skills necessary to design and implement these innovations. Progress can be made in many of the theoretical and practical areas outlined above. To achieve this, a large part of our energies will need to be devoted to shaping up appropriate behaviours in policy-makers and resource allocators.

8 THE EMPLOYMENT OF CLINICAL PSYCHOLOGISTS: PRESENT AND FUTURE

M. P. Feldman

In this chapter I shall look at possible future patterns of employment in clinical psychology in the light both of current trends and of the actions which clinical psychologists might take themselves. Although I will be concerned with the clinical area of professional psychology, some of my assertions have implications for other areas also. One of the main conclusions that I shall reach is that the present professional divisions are unsatisfactory and artificial both in employment and in training.

Clinical Service Posts in the NHS

The profession of clinical psychology is a young one, the majority of its members being under 35. For the next 20 to 25 years there will be relatively little attrition due to retirement. However, because the profession includes a significant proportion of women, at least half the current output from training courses, many of whom either leave entirely for some years to start a family or work part-time during those years, the turnover of jobs is a little higher than it would have been in an all-male profession. Moreover, there is something of a movement overseas (Feldman, 1980) but this seems to have been largely confined to Australia (Canada and the USA require a doctorate) and that country is now restricting professional immigration. The ease of movement between the EEC countries does provide an alternative destination, but this may well be balanced by a move into Britain of psychologists from the Community. In general then, assuming that the present situation is maintained whereby about 75 to 100 new clinical psychologists per year will seek employment in the NHS, and that sources of clinical employment alternative to the NHS do not open up, the current number of NHS clinical psychologists will increase from the present 850 or so in 1978 (Barden, 1979) to well over 2,000 before a significant reduction occurs due to retirement. The total number of new posts needed over the next 20 years would be about 1,200, perhaps more. There are two obstacles in the way of the suggested increase, financial resources and the attitude of other professions, principally medicine.

Both may be serious. First, to employ between 75 and 100 additional NHS clinical psychologists per year would cost at least an additional £1,000,000 annually (including support services). This does not seem too difficult, given that the mental health and mental handicap areas (and that of geriatrics, an important future setting for clinical psychology employment), largely under-resourced for many years, are intended to secure a much larger share than in the past, both of any new monies and of old monies available for redistribution. However, new monies do seem very unlikely, and any shift of resources will be strongly resisted by those in other areas of care (i.e. outside mental health, etc.).

The second obstacle, that put up by other mental health professionals, may be of even more importance. In the last decade there has been a major shift in the role of NHS clinical psychologists. They now have major responsibilities for programmes of treatment in the fields of mental handicap, sexual problems, and a broad range of the psychological problems of adults and children which lie outside the scope of effective interventions by biological means such as chemotherapy, surgery or ECT. Very broadly, clinical psychologists, irrespective of orientation, would agree that a first degree in psychology, followed by professional training in clinical psychology is a better preparation for dealing with the problems listed above, than a basic qualification in medicine, with its — quite correct — emphasis on applied biology, and a further training in psychiatry, the specifically psychological content of which is typically limited. With the exception of some of the major teaching centres this important and rapid expansion of role has encountered relatively little overt resistance from psychiatrists for a number of reasons, including the sheer size of the therapeutic task, the lack of training of most psychiatrists in psychological methods of treatment — both behavioural and psychodynamic — and a preference of some for organic approaches. Moreover, a considerable proportion of those occupying junior posts in psychiatry have been from overseas countries, many of whom may have seen their stay in this country as temporary, for training purposes only, and so had less at stake in defending professional territory than if they saw their long-term careers in Britain. There are no hard data on this point, but it is instructive to make a subjective comparison between the degree of professional freedom open to a department of clinical psychology in a major London teaching hospital and one in a provincial mental or general hospital. Most clinical psychologists work in the latter sector. Will this continue, with clinical psychologists more and more replacing psychiatrists in the 'non-organic' area? I have been assured by more than one senior figure in clinical psychology that this indeed will occur, that psychiatry, like capitalism, will simply 'wither away' gradually, the transition being quite painless.

There is reason to believe, however, that the present relative acquiescence of psychiatrists in the expanding role of clinical psychology may be a temporary phenomenon, with the demarcation issue being far from settled in our favour. A look at the number of students currently training in British medical schools helps to support this note of caution: several new medical schools have opened recently, the existing schools have increased their intake sharply and the total output will reach nearly 4,000 by the early 1980s (a few years ago it was only 2,500). The BMA is already making warning noises about 'medical unemployment'; their anxiety enhanced by the reduced opportunities for emigration to the USA and Canada. Medical output is high in most of the EEC countries, so that opportunities in Europe are unlikely to mop up the increased output of British doctors. So far as academically measured quality is concerned, the A-level grades currently required by medical schools are easily the highest of any of the science-based disciplines, at least three Bs. Psychology typically asks for three Cs or less (the balance is at least righted by the high quality of the small percentage of psychology graduates able to enter training in clinical psychology). If we project forward about ten years we can envisage a rapid filling up, first of vacancies in the more popular medical areas (of which, it should be noted, general practice is now one), and then of the less popular ones (geriatrics, psychiatry, perhaps even mental handicap). The large number of overseas-trained doctors in junior psychiatric posts will be replaced by British-trained doctors of high intellectual calibre, committed to the search for consultant posts in this country. Will they be content with the 'organic' area of psychological problems? The answer depends in part on whether NHS-based clinical psychology, in the next ten years, can establish itself fairly unassailably in the 'non-organic' area, not only by continuing the present pace of research advances and practical applications, but by actively seeking genuine responsibility — and that means legal responsibility. If we fail to do so, my prediction is that psychiatry will make a real attempt to roll back the considerable professional advances made by clinical psychology in the past decade. The restricted role still available to clinical psychologists in a few of the more resistant teaching hospitals might well be seen by psychiatrists as the desirable model for the mental health field in general.

The Trethowan Report (1977) partially blurred the demarcation dispute by advocating the 'team approach'. 'Relations between psychologists and members of other health service professions should be based on mutually beneficial teamwork' (Trethowan, 1977). However, anyone who does clinical work with problems treated by psychological methods, as opposed for example to those requiring surgery, knows that the 'team' idea is largely a polite fiction. Psychological treatment is either one-to-one, one-to-a-group, or some variation involving intermediate levels of manpower as in the triadic model, in which the psychologist trains another professional (nurse, probation officer, etc.) who then works with the actual client/family in the natural environment (Tharp and Wetzel, 1969). The common feature is that treatment programmes are initiated and monitored by a single specialist in the development and management of psychological problems. If there is indeed a team it is very clear that it has a leader and that the leader should be the expert in the academic/clinical discipline basic to the problem area, in this case clinical psychology. When treatment is by an 'organic' method the leader or sole practitioner involved is a medically qualified person. This may seem a blunt view of the situation, but I feel sure that it expresses the views of many of those clinical psychologists who have qualified since the shift occurred towards an enlarged professional role. (I remember well my own continued doubts about working without 'medical cover'; in retrospect they seem absurd.) The assumption of full professional and legal responsibility for one's professional work would not be unique; it has already happened in the case of social workers and probation officers, and even nearer home in that of educational psychologists. It would be most unwise to wait for another ten years and for another review of clinical psychologists in the NHS. Instead, the profession should immediately invest time and effort into an enquiry into the legal foundations of clinical responsibility currently vested by the NHS in doctors. My impression is that this would repay careful examination. The present medical view was expressed very clearly by the Trethowan Report; 'we fully recognise that for any patient under treatment in the National Health Service there is a continually medical responsibility which cannot be handed over to any other profession' (Trethowan, 1977). Taken together with the above statement on 'teamwork', it is very clear that Trethowan intended a continued medical pre-eminence in responsibility. It is desirable to press on as rapidly as possible with the present moves towards professional registration and the establishment of a College of Applied Psychology. The two developments are closely related and would help to provide the statutory bases for professional and legal responsibility by the NHS clinical psychologists.

In general, clinical psychologists would be sensible not to put all their eggs into the NHS basket, although it is likely that the majority will continue to be employed in that sector. I have indicated elsewhere (Feldman, 1980) that small numbers of Birmingham-trained clinical psychologists take employment after training in a range of other contexts, including teaching and research and in several non-NHS clinical settings, including student health centres, community homes, local authority social services departments, and even in voluntary agencies. The same is likely to be true of those graduating from other courses. I shall discuss these areas of employment below, beginning with the voluntary sector, both because it is less well known than the others and because it may have wider implications for the assumption of professional and legal responsibility.

Clinical Psychologists in the Voluntary Sector

I shall illustrate the voluntary sector with two examples of which I have personal experience.

Aquarius came into being following my receipt of a research grant from a Birmingham charitable trust for a study into hostel-based services for alcoholics. Hugh Norris, a clinical psychologist appointed to direct the programme of research which is being carried out by Alcoholics Rehabilitation Research Group (ARRG), came to the crucial conclusion that it was unsatisfactory simply to monitor existing services: the staff concerned would be understandably reluctant to set up new comparative programmes, or even to engage in lengthy sessions of questionnaire completion. The alternative, setting up new hostels in which relatively clear-cut treatment programmes could be carried out and monitored by specially recruited and trained staff, required that we establish a new voluntary agency. This could receive statutory funding from both central and local government, and purchase, equip and run hostels, taking full responsibility for the clients. Dr Norris took up his research appointment in January 1975. Aquarius was set up about a year later, with Dr Norris as Chairman and moving spirit and myself as Treasurer. After many initial problems — essentially we had to learn our way round a completely new world — Aquarius is now well established. It has four centres: hostels in Birmingham, Wolverhampton and Northampton, which provide between them over 40 places, and a

Day Centre in Birmingham, which can serve over 20 clients at any one time. To date ARRG/Aquarius combined have employed four clinical psychologists and several psychology graduates in more junior posts, all of whom have worked in the hostels or day centres and have been fully responsible under Hugh Norris's overall direction for their professional work of helping people with drinking and related problems. Even after the completion of the present ARRG project it is certain that Aquarius will continue as a voluntary agency in the field of alcoholism, of medium size by comparison with other such organisations, with a very strong commitment to clinical psychology. This will ensure the continuity of Aquarius' present policy of employing clinical psychologists, among other professionals, to provide a service explicitly based on the findings of psychology and with a strong emphasis on measurement and evaluation.

Shape has a less clear-cut history. After existing for some years as a voluntary agency concerned with the social rehabilitation of young offenders the Trustees sought the advice of Ian Reid, then Senior Clinical Psychologist at All Saint's Hospital, Birmingham, and formerly a Home Office Prison Psychologist, specialising in the young offender group. Mr Reid set up a behaviourally-based programme of social skills training and was instrumental in arranging for the Shape Trustees and Committee of Management to be augmented by several members of staff of the University of Birmingham with an interest in criminological research and/or the care of young offenders. The Shape programme is described in some detail by Reid, Feldman and Ostapuik (1980) (see also Chapter 7). Once again, the presence on the committee of the voluntary agency of psychologists and others from related and sympathetic disciplines ensures the continued employment of clinical psychologists and, most important, of the methods of the discipline. As in the case of Aquarius, research and evaluation are fully integral with the service component. Thus far, Shape is established only in Birmingham and only on a residential basis.

Both Aquarius and Shape may well extend further: the framework exists. Now that they are sufficiently well developed to do so, both agencies serve as clinical attachments for Birmingham MSc/PhD students. I have mentioned Aquarius and Shape because there are other examples in the voluntary sector of alternatives to the more usual forms of clinical employment. (As a final cautionary note it should be said that the great advantages of the voluntary sector are partially balanced by the financial position being rather less secure than that of the public sector agencies!)

Other Work Settings for Clinical Psychologists

A number of articles have appeared in the *Bulletin of the BPS*, including
an account of the North East London Polytechnic (NELP) teaching
clinic (Hallam and Liddell, 1978), local authority community psychology (Bender, 1979a) and work in family practitioner health centres
(e.g. McPherson and Feldman, 1977). In addition, several clinical
psychologists work in university or higher education health centres.
For example, the Student Health Centre at the University of Birmingham now has an establishment of two clinical psychologists and has
served for several years as a training centre for the Birmingham MSc/
PhD course. Essentially, this psychological service is part of a group
general practice, though funded through the University and not the
local Family Practitioner Committee. Many students (and members of
staff) refer themselves, other referrals are from tutors, the doctors of
the group practice, and the University Department of Psychiatry.

Psychological work in the Birmingham University Health Centre and
in the NELP clinic might well serve as partial models for agencies
serving self-referring populations, treated non-residentially, for problems
across the whole non-organic range. (Aquarius and Shape are specialist
in content and are largely residential.) Both, however, have a
specialised purpose (training in the case of NELP, and service to a
particular population in the case of university health centres). The next
step might be a voluntary agency offering the full range of psychological services to the population at large on a self-referring non-
residential basis.

A very limited and tentative experiment, the Clinical Psychology
Centre, which borrows from and builds on the NELP teaching clinic
(Hallam and Liddell, 1978), has just started at the Department of
Psychology, University of Birmingham. Initially, the Centre will offer
a limited psychological service to clients referred by a small number of
local GPs with whom the clinical psychology lecturers of the department have had a continuing and long-standing involvement. Next we
will invite, again on a limited basis, referrals from a range of voluntary
agencies. Finally, after all has gone satisfactorily with the first two
stages, we will offer the opportunity of self-referral to the general
public. There is to be no duplication of existing NHS facilities or
services, or referral from them, with the exception of the initial small
group of GPs. Inevitably the scale of the 'Centre' will remain small.
The four clinical lecturers concerned can devote only a limited amount
of time and the main, indeed over-riding purpose, as in the case of the

NELP Clinic, is to provide training in clinical skills to the students taking our MSc/PhD in Clinical Psychology for whom the Centre will be one of a large number of possible attachments. However, the very existence of the Centre, albeit limited, will serve, together with the NELP Clinic, as an experimental demonstration of a different model of clinical responsibility from that asserted for clinical psychology in the Trethowan Report, particularly as the Centre will be open to clinical psychologists employed outside the university, mainly in the West Midlands Regional Health Authority. All 'users' of the Centre will concentrate on trying out new approaches to helping clients and on methods of carrying them out, as well as the development of services to novel client groups.

The next step might be a voluntary agency which builds on the NELP Clinic and the University of Birmingham Centre. It would, however, emphasise a service, rather than a training role, and would be housed in a busy central shopping area of the city rather than in a higher education campus so as to allow the greatest possible ease of access for potential clients. (Ironically, such services already exist in the form of voluntary agencies such as the Samaritans, the Marriage Guidance Council and so on. They are essentially non-professional, in the sense of an absence of formal training and qualifications and they offer their services largely free. While they frequently refer on to professional care agencies, they do seem to provide much counselling and other support. It seems not unreasonable to assert that if amateurs can function independently, so can professionals!) It is likely that people often seek help for an area of concern which is intertwined very closely with those in other areas and it would therefore be sensible for a 'psychological help' agency to be housed together with and to co-operate very closely with, agencies supplying expert advice in a range of the other personal difficulties, such as legal, housing and consumer affairs.

What might be the financial base of the psychological component of such a 'broad spectrum' personal help and advice agency? There seem several possibilities. First, psychologists might operate as an 'outreach' of the university/poly-based clinic staffed by clinical psychology academic staff and postgraduate students. Secondly, clients might pay a modest fee so as to encourage the provision of services by psychologists other than those whose major responsibility is towards training. Thirdly, voluntary agencies can be registered as charitable bodies with consequent access to trusts and other grant-giving organisations. Fourthly, there are, even in these times of reduced public expenditure, various statutory funds from both local and central government which are available to voluntary agencies, particularly those breaking new ground (e.g. Joint Financing, Inner City Partnership, etc.). Aquarius and Shape provide examples: both employ psychologists and other professionals and both obtain a majority of their funding from local and central government.

Eventually, we might envisage a statutory body, separate from the NHS, providing services across the full range of personal (non-medical) care. It could be argued that in principle such bodies already exist in the shape of local authority social services departments, but they have so far done relatively little outside certain special client groups, mainly the elderly, children in difficulties and some of the handicapped. The majority of the large population outside these categories has its psychological services provided by the NHS. Moreover, social services departments are strongly oriented towards provisions for the poor and there is a strong case for social workers continuing to concentrate on these very necessary functions.

Coping with Problems Where They Occur

Thus far, in discussing where psychologists might offer their services, I have followed the current convention whereby most clients 'bring' their problem to the psychologist who sees them in hospital, clinic, office, etc., and not the social context in which the problem occurs — home, workplace and so on. The alternative approach, that of coping with the problem in its own natural environment, was set out some years ago by Tharp and Wetzel (1969), as follows: 'The environment in which the individual is embedded is principally responsible for the organisation, or disorganisation, the maintenance or change, the appearance or disappearance, of any behaviour.' It follows that inter- vention and prevention should occur in the individual's 'natural environment' (family, school, friendship group, workplace, etc.) and not in the artificial environment of the helping centre.

From time to time, but far from routinely, psychologists do visit clients in their own homes (admittedly, this is rather time-consuming), but do so very infrequently indeed in their workplaces. Yet many female adults under 60 and almost all male adults under 65 spend at least half of their waking lives at work. Many of their psychological problems occur in work settings and should be dealt with there. Large- scale organisations, both public and private, already employ occupational psychologists. It seems a reasonable guess that as research proceeds with the methods of coping with occupational stress (e.g.

Broadbent, 1980; Robinson, 1978) such organisations will also employ clinical psychologists. Perhaps, the two branches of applied psychology might see a mutual advantage in some sharing of training facilities and skills. This point, of the essential indivisibility of applied psychology, is taken up in the section on training.

Teaching and Research

For an earlier generation of clinical psychologists teaching and research were as important a source of employment as the NHS (Drewe, 1971). The present generation is much less likely to go into teaching and research, but they still attract between 10 and 15 per cent of the total output (Williams, 1980; Feldman, 1980). At least this has been so during the past ten years. What of the future? A personal guess is that we have reached a plateau both in clinical courses and in student numbers. Unless student–staff ratios improve, the present, typically young, clinical teaching staff will need only a few replacements annually (providing that they do not move into the NHS, always possible unless pay disparities diminish). The same applies to clinical psychologists in departments of psychiatry, although some development in staffing may still occur as the 'behavioural science' content of the more slowly changing medical schools increases in line with the current fashion. My impression is that many of the undergraduate departments of psychology not associated with a clinical psychology course now have a clinically trained lecturer on their staff; some further appointments may occur. Other academic departments occasionally appoint psychologists, for example, architecture, and faculties of law may do so (as in the USA) but there is no special niche in either for clinical psychologists over and above other psychology specialisms. So far as research is concerned, the career prospects for clinical psychologists have never been very good. The major employer is the Medical Research Council and the career structure is such as to provide few opportunities for clinical psychologists at the senior level. There seems much medical resistance to research units in which the directorship is earmarked for a clinical psychologist, and even to filling such posts on an open basis. This is another area in which the profession ought to be taking a substantial political interest.

All of this is not to say that clinical psychology training courses should neglect teaching and research. On the contrary, both will occupy a substantial portion of the time of most clinical psychologists, particularly when they are aggregated into departments of substantial size, allowing some degree of specialisation, or at least rotation between

specialities. To this end, all clinical courses are, rightly, encouraged by
the Division of Clinical Psychology to emphasise training in teaching
and in research methods, and I would like to see this emphasis
extended in the future. While many clinical psychologists will prefer
to be solely practitioners, or practitioner-teachers, it is very desirable
that others should become practitioner-scientist-teachers. It does seem
likely that the majority of clinical research will be carried out by those
employed basically as clinical psychologists, rather than as full-time
researchers.

Operating on a Wider Scale – the Community Approach

The term 'community psychology' has been used in at least two major
ways. The less radical version is represented by the above discussion on
clinical psychology practised outside the National Health Service, but
still interventionist rather than preventive in nature. That is, the
psychologists waits until help is sought – until a problem is apparent.
A number of ways in which psychologists offer help involve working
through others rather than direct client contact, but are still essentially
interventionist. One example is the triadic model, another is the use of
non-professionals, as when the psychologist takes as treatment partners,
the parents of handicapped children who then continue the intervention
over a longer period. A third method of using scarce psychological
resources more cost-effectively is to involve 'buddies' or volunteer
workers. Detailed reviews of such approaches can be found in Feldman
and Orford (1980). The more radical approach confines 'community
psychology' to preventive work. Many reports have been given of
attempts at primary prevention (that is to prevent the occurrence of
problems before they even begin to appear, and aimed at a whole
population or sub-population). The results to date vary somewhat but
seem rather promising in the fields of parent and teacher training
(Herbert, 1980), handicap (Cowen, 1980) and physical health – such
as the reduction of cardiac risk factors through mass-media campaigns
(McGuire, 1980).

Good environmental design may also contribute to the prevention of
psychological problems in general, for example by breaking up larger
units into smaller ones in schools and housing projects (O'Donnell,
1980). The effect is to increase opportunities for social participation:
it seems that close social networks of personal friends are of great
importance in coping with the inevitable stresses and strains of life.
The formation of such networks is assisted both by appropriate
environmental design and hence access to potential friends and by

social skills in friendship formation and maintenance, so that providing opportunities to develop social skills might be included in the list of possible preventive exercises. Clearly, the prevention approach takes us well outside the conventional professional roles and skills of the clinical psychologist, a point amplified in the section on training. Moreover, ensuring effective prevention implies gaining access to those who formulate political and economic policy, and hence the development of a range of organisational skills very different from those appropriate to client care.

Primary prevention holds out two great hopes: more effective help and less expensive help. There can be little doubt, whichever government is in power, that the test of cost-effectiveness will be applied with increasing rigour, and that special pleading and political clout will play a diminishing, though still important part. Psychologists cannot hope to be very strong in the latter area: in the long run we shall only maintain and strengthen our position if what we offer survives the test of cost-effectiveness. This means a continuing commitment to clinical research, both in training and in the service context, to which evaluation should be built-in, and a constant search for methods of delivering psychological services as cheaply as possible, without loss of effectiveness.

Implications for Training

The Content and Structure of Courses

If my speculations about future employment are correct the range of professional tasks for the clinical psychologist of the future will be much wider than at present, from departments of psychology in the NHS, through other methods of delivering intervention services, to posts in social agencies planning and executing large-scale programmes of prevention. The inevitable consequence will be that compared with the present position considerably more areas of 'basic' psychology will be drawn upon and a greater range of skills will need to be taught. The extension in both academic bases and applications will be such as to cross the traditional boundaries between the branches of applied psychology. For example, the effective use of the mass media for communication programmes aimed at primary prevention requires at least as much acquaintance with the methods and findings of social psychology as with those of clinical psychology. The possibility of dealing with occupational stress implies that clinical psychologists should have some training in occupational psychology, and vice versa. Exactly the same could be said for the interdependence of clinical and educational psychologists in dealing with children's problems, whether at home or at school. A logical end point is a single profession of applied psychology, with a basic training followed by specialisation, which can draw on the full range of psychological research and applications. There are major difficulties against the achievement of such an end-point, however desirable, constraints of different geographical locations, historically-based variations in length of course and teaching emphases, and territorial defensiveness. Yet at the very least it seems worthwhile for the different professional groups to examine jointly the pattern of likely future employment and the associated requirements for professional training, so as to seek unification wherever possible. The very hopeful signs in the meanwhile are the proposals, under serious consideration by the British Psychological Society, of a College of Applied Psychology and a register of professional psychologists.

There are also implications for the academic content of training for applied psychology of a move from the clinic/office/hospital into workplaces/homes and from a back-room role 'servicing' other professions into one involving interaction with political and economic decision-takers. In addition to a thorough grounding in the biological, social and individual experience components of behaviour, applied psychologists of the future must have an appreciation of what can be borrowed from sociology, social anthropology, social geography and economics and political science. This means not only communicating with other applied psychologists but also with other professions, a theme already exemplified by a most imaginative graduate programme being conducted at the State University of New York by Professor Krasner and associates, ranging across a number of fields from psychology to architecture (Krasner, in press).

The changes in psychological practice that I have set out as both desirable and at least potentially possible are obviously enormous. Yet many of us in clinical psychology have experienced in the recent past changes almost as massive. No doubt the same is true for the other branches of applied psychology. The time scale does not have to go back very far. Norris (1978), now a principal psychologist in the West Midlands, has recalled his experiences as a probationary NHS psychologist in 1967. His day consisted largely of routine testing, typically unrelated to any therapeutic procedures, and sitting through reviews of patients at which the information discussed was of the most broad and vague kind. Today it is very unusual for a student not to be given in his first year a significant responsibility for the treatment of many clients. By the end of the second year of training he will have had treatment experience in a number of settings, ranging from the student health centre to a traditional long-stay ward. There have been associated changes on the academic side of training. Very little resemblance can be found between the detailed academic content of the Birmingham Clinical Course when it started in 1967 and the present syllabus. We have cut back very sharply on psychological assessment, both basic principles and the details of individual tests, and on psychiatric and other medical teaching. The weight of teaching in psychological therapies has increased greatly. We have introduced courses in such professional skills as management and a large number of second year options: geropsychology, psychophysiology, community psychology, criminal behaviour, social aspects of psychological problems, and others, the bulk of the references given to students being post 1970 and even post 1975.

Funding and Higher Qualifications

I have argued that it would be very desirable for a substantial minority of clinical psychologists to seek employment outside conventional NHS settings and I have sketched a number of possibilities. Further, it would be desirable in the longer run to end the demarcation between professional psychologists, both in employment and in training. What form might be taken by the funding of a generic programme of training? One clear implication is that funding should be central, administered through a single research council, rather than through the present patchwork of health authorities and MRC (clinical), SSRC (occupational), local education authorities and the central training pool (educational), and self funding (all specialisations). Trainees would be regarded and paid as postgraduate students preparing for a single unified profession through generic schemes of training with special options. I have no doubt that there would be strenuous objections from a number of interested parties, such as the relevant trade unions. However, the latter might reflect that there is nothing to stop postgraduate students from joining unions — many are now members of ASTMS.

There would also be the problem of the BPS Diploma, which would have to be replaced totally by university courses (studentships can only be held by those in training at universities/polytechnics). This is not as drastic as it might appear: in the clinical area at least the BPS diploma was originally conceived of as a temporary staging post on the way to a solely university-based system of training. Moreover, the projected College of Applied Psychology would enable the profession to establish more advanced, *post-training* professional qualifications, somewhat on the line of the diplomas administered by the American Board of Examiners in Professional Psychology. These are awarded in several areas of professional psychology for the formally assessed demonstration of professional skills well beyond the basic qualification (in America, typically the doctorate).

Central funding at the postgraduate studentship level, administered by a single research council and applied to generic courses has a number of advantages. First, it enables central planning and the more efficient use of scarce training resources. Secondly, it supports and strengthens the unified nature of the psychological profession. Thirdly, by removing funding from control by the prospective employer it would encourage psychologists to enter a much wider range of employment than at present. Central funding of the type suggested is thus an essential component of the major theme of this chapter — the move towards an independent, and unified profession of applied psychology, employed in a very wide range of settings.

WHOSE PSYCHOLOGY? SOME ISSUES IN THE SOCIAL CONTROL OF PSYCHOLOGICAL PRACTICE

Andrew Sutton

The bulk of psychological practice in the United Kingdom is conducted within the public service. There exists a small number of client-serving psychologists in private practice. Rather more perhaps work for voluntarily funded agencies, and there are numerous instances of psychologists' doing occasional private work on the side. The social effects of this tiny private sector, however, remain negligible. There also exists a relatively small number of public-service psychologists, working for the armed and civil services, whose work relates more to the ergonomic and occupational concerns of their employing institutions rather than presenting an explicit, direct commitment to the personal welfare of citizens. They will not be considered further here. The dominant image of present-day professional psychological practice in this country is provided by the large numbers (nearly 2,000 in all) of clinical and educational psychologists working for the National Health Service and the local authorities. Whatever specific differences there are between the two sub-groups, they present a common face in their salaried employment by major institutions of the state, their agreed (or at least conventional) minimal entry require-ments involving 'professional' training at postgraduate level, and their membership of the 'helping professions'. One might add that the bulk of them are young (mid-20s to mid-30s), that perhaps the majority are humane and concerned to better the lot of their fellow citizens, and that much of their practice is directed to the successors of what Midwinter (1977) has called 'the four unpresentable and unprepo-ssessing "P's" of the Victorian populace — paupers, pupils, patients and prisoners'.

Much of our current psychological theory and practice hail from the United States. Psychologists in this country are generally aware, however, that a considerable proportion of American psychological practice, certainly a much larger proportion than is the case here, is undertaken outside of the public system. We are correspondingly relieved at our freedom from the constraints and pressures of the private sector, bestowed by the public ownership of the means of

psychological production in the United Kingdom. Yet while psychological practice as a primarily public service is doubtless in many
respects a liberal and progressive social provision, bringing psychology
and its possible benefits to all irrespective of the ability to pay, we
must recognise that the provision of psychological services *via* public
institutions, and especially the near monopoly of the public sector in
this field, raise important questions, both about the actual social role
of psychology in this country and about the nature of our psychology
itself.

The attention that can be devoted to these questions here will focus
upon the practice of psychology for local government, a practice
largely involving children and especially their interactions with the
formal education system. Educational psychologists, who constitute
most (though no longer quite all) of this provision, have a long history
of public service practice, and especially since the NHS Reorganisation
Act (1973) they have acquired extensive experience of the pressures of
the real world, unprotected by the medical umbrella. In this country
then, as perhaps in the United States (see Barden, 1977) the
experiences of educational psychologists may serve as a basis for
determining what might lie ahead for other areas of psychological
practice. Clinical psychologists and others may seek parallels to their
own experience or point to differences as they please – they should,
however, at least consider the problems encountered by the largest
and longest established group of psychological practitioners, and the
one with the most substantial experience of working 'in the
community'.

Public-service psychological practice was typified above as 'client-
serving'. Being simultaneously a public servant and a 'help agent' raises
the immediate dilemma of 'who is the client?' The local authority
psychologist is a 'servant of the authority', his work being frequently
described as 'a service to the schools' or 'a service to teachers'. When
(s)he is dealing with an individual child or family (s)he cannot in
reality offer the direct, professionally responsible, personal relationship
of mutual trust, supposedly enjoyed by doctor and patient, even though
the psychologist–client relationship might be offered and outwardly
conducted as if such a carefully defined and safeguarded situation
existed here too. The psychologist–client relationship is honest and
secure only as long as no conflicts of loyalty occur: as soon as the
interests of the employing authority (or powerful forces within it)
come into conflict with those of the client, then there arises the very
real risk that the client's right of advocacy (Sutton, 1977) are in

jeopardy. Local authority psychologists have no direct access to the community at large. Their terms of service do not permit them to campaign publicly against inadequacies or iniquities that they know mar the school system of which they are a part, in the way, for example, that medical specialists are free to expose the flaws in the health service. Local authority psychologists have contact with the community mediated by their employer in all but at the individual clinical level (and in a few really restrictive authorities even at that level too). Local authority employees do not sign the Official Secrets Act, but they still effectively surrender their rights as citizens to speak and act on matters that might deeply concern them, about which they might be uniquely informed, and which may encompass issues of potentially grave public concern. Public debate over 'sensitive' questions of educational policy and practice (behaviour problems, school illiteracy, and/or incompetent teachers and heads, school organisation, teacher training, etc.) has been notably lacking in contributions from those psychologists who, in fairly large numbers now, spend their working days embroiled in such issues. This is not because local authority psychologists are so universally lacking in talent or concern as to have nothing to say on these matters. Teachers make their voices heard, through their powerful and vocal trade unions: the psychologists, however, remain unheard, because they are powerless in the face of the constraints of the workplace.

Many local authority psychologists feel that their duties ought to lie first and foremost towards their clients (whom they would regard as comprising children and families), their own views of what is socially just, and their integrity as scientists — and only secondly towards their employing institutions. It seems likely that most parents who have dealings with psychologists might be expected to assume that psychologists would be free to think, *and act*, according to some such system of values, within the general bounds of the law. It seems equally likely that most local authorities would take it most amiss if their psychologists (or any other employees) did indeed think, *and act*, according to such priorities. The law, however, is fairly clear (McCartney and O'Mahony, 1977): a contract exists between a psychologist and his client only in the setting of private practice and, like it or not, in normal circumstances the contract exists between client and the psychologist's employer. The psychologist's responsibilities to the client exist within this framework. As has been argued elsewhere (Sutton, 1976; 1978a) local authority psychologists are employed primarily to serve the local authority, and only secondarily their individual clients,

the community in which they live or the scientific discipline of
psychology, for to work in any other way would be to step beyond the
limits of their particular professionalism and unilaterally abrogate
responsibilities that the local authority regards as its own: it would
moreover make the activities of the authority visible, and therefore
potentially accountable, and cause conflict (usually conceived of as
'trouble') amongst other sub-groups within and around the authority.
The particular 'bureau-professionalism' that educational psychology
has negotiated within local government as its precarious professional
base is no different from that of other local authority helping
professions in this respect. Other psychological practitioners in the
public service who wish to throw stones ought to examine the basis of
their own professionalisms (say in the manner of Fielding and
Portwood, 1980) to see how differently they themselves might be
placed, or how similarly.

The 'traditional' view of any moral dilemmas that educational
psychologists might feel about the ownership of their labour has been
that they already have a ready-made system of ethics in the ethics of
the education system (whatever they might be). This reckoning might
have indeed been valid when educational psychologists' allegiances
were still 'educational'. A *doyen* of English educational psychology,
Wright (1974), has suggested that conflicts of loyalty are rare anyway,
since ' . . . local education authorities exist to help the individual, so
the ultimate goal is the same'. A quite contrary view, and its implications for psychological practice, has been argued by no less august
figures in American school psychology (Hyman and Schrieber, 1975):
'[we] recognise bureaucracies as the major institutional force in
depersonalisation and denying human rights'. Whatever else has been
imported from American school psychology, the intense concern with
children's and families' rights in the face of the bureaucracies of schools
and school boards that abounds in the American school psychology
journals, has found scant public reflection amongst British educational
psychologists. Barden (1977) has characterised American school
psychology over the seventies in the following terms.

There is little quarrel that legal, ethical and moral considerations
have been the predominant determinants, at least during the past
five to seven years, in shifts in what school psychologists do and
how they go about doing it . . .
. . . the burden of providing services while involved in the
entanglements of legal, moral, ethical and bureaucratic quagmires,

seems sometimes to have almost stopped effective services to children, teachers and schools.

Note that many American school psychologists have themselves taken an active public part in the hard-fought political campaigns over, for example, integration, mainstreaming, handicapped rights, corporal punishment, and the psychometric examination of minority-group children, that brought the above situation about in the first place. Over the same period many educational psychologists in this country have espoused the same causes, but have not taken up the same tools to achieve them. If they wish it, their work may be largely spared explicit legal, moral and ethical entanglements, and their major bureaucratic quagmire is contained in the 'SE Procedures' (Department of Education and Science, 1975) for securing places in special schools. Note that educational psychologists as a body *did* invest considerable (largely behind-the-scenes) effort in the establishment of these procedures, and that many still regard them as a significant step forward in the advance of their professionalism.

The traditional, consensus view of an identity of interest between employer and psychologist (including often too, negotiable common interests with other interested professional groups, the child and family, society at large and its wider institutions) may just about hold together for many of the cases that local authority psychologists deal with, and perhaps where involvement remains superficial for a considerable proportion. But it would be an odd view of social reality that upheld the possibility of such equanimity in anything like *all* problems, asserting that the interests of individuals or groups can always be pursued without detracting from the interests of other groups or individuals. There will inevitably arise occasions when the interest of client or society will clash with those of school or local authority, or even with the personal interests of the psychologist or the professional aspirations of psychologists as a group. It is in these cases involving conflict that concepts like 'professional integrity' are truly put to the test, rather than in those where there is achieved an apparent community of interest amongst all participants, and this remains so whatever the relative proportions of the two different situations within psychologists' workloads. It should not be considered slighting to point out that where there is conflict it is often 'professional integrity' that is the first to go. Psychologists are after all only human: they have the same preferences for unstressful working lives and secure jobs as do most other people in our society, and now more than at any other time in the history of psychological practice they do not want to find themselves unemployed with the possibility of never working again. In Ingleby's (1975) words, 'their activities have become industries and those who staff these industries are a new proletariat, who (like the rest) must submit to being used in order to stay alive'. The realities of professionalism and the ethics of all the state 'helping professions' lie in this ownership of our work.

It is well to remember, however, that in one respect psychological practice faces unique problems, because psychology stands at the intersection of the helping professions with 'science'. If the practising psychologist is to retain his status as a scientist, rather than to be simply a purveyor of ideas and techniques developed by other psychologists, then (s)he has an obligation to undertake scientific work, research. Haywood (1976) has discussed the implications of such a position in his own field, mental retardation.

> The theme . . . is simple: while psychologists may be guilty of unethical conduct if they conduct research in ways that could bring harm to their subjects of such magnitude that the potential risks outweigh the benefits to be realised from the research, psychologists may also be guilty of unethical conduct if they fail to conduct important research. The latter part of the statement may be especially true of psychologists who work in areas such as mental retardation, that are so characterised by ignorance that the systematic acquisition of new knowledge is especially critical.

Amongst the legion of problems met in psychological practice for local government there seems no reason to single out mental retardation as a field especially 'characterised by ignorance'. They all are. New knowledge is desperately needed, but the psychologist might find his activity so blocked by established professional or bureaucratic interests that there may be no choice but to continue to behave, in Haywood's sense 'unethically', by allowing the ignorance and the practices based upon it to continue unabated. The dilemma from the psychologist's point of view is then whether to withdraw from such areas altogether, or to continue to work with them at a marginal level. To continue to do so may not necessarily be a helpful or even a neutral act: it might serve as a collusive recognition of the legitimacy of procedures that are at best untested, and which may well be outrightly harmful. From the employing authority's point of view, a psychologist has been appointed to service a particular system (child guidance, special schools placement, social services assessment) that other psychologists may well have contributed to urging on them in the first place. Now (s)he wants to find a 'better' way of going about matters, one that has profound effects upon a whole range of associated systems and locally established reputations. Psychologists whose ethical system includes being scientists as well as help agents, will always be at risk of biting the hands that feed them, or so it would seem to their employers. Institutions tend to resist strife and change: it is therefore not just psychologists' client-directed activity that needs to be controlled, it is also their science.

The wage-relationship provides part of this control. Psychologists who visibly cannot, or will not, offer a particular kind of psychology in the first place will not be employed, but as the recent industrial tribunal involving an educational psychologist has shown, a local authority psychologist in post may be relieved of his employment if, among other reasons, his psychology does not fit (' . . . for failure to conform to his employer's instructions . . . for example, by failing to conduct and record tests', quoted from the *Decision of the Industrial Tribunal. . . .* , 1978). The authority's rights of ownership also stretch to the material manifestations of the psychologist's work: reports, notes, etc. are the property of the employer, who can legally require them to be handed over (see also McCartney and O'Mahoney, 1977). But however dissatisfied or disgruntled many local authority psychologists may sometimes feel about aspects of their work, it remains exceedingly rare for one to step so far out of line that the economic and legal power of the employer need be openly invoked. This is in part a factor of a certain tolerance within local government, particularly for the activities of the 'professional person' or the exercise of 'professional judgement'. In part, however, another mechanism is in play, one which operates to maintain a high degree of self-regulation amongst all the helping professionals, but which has particular implications for the psychologist and for the development of psychological science.

The dominant groupings and institutions in society possess not only much of society's material goods, but also much of its cultural apparatus. They provide for our use, amongst other things, concepts of what is 'professional', 'scientific', 'responsible', 'ethical', etc. so that it can be difficult even to recognise that there are potentially other psychologies that might be generated for the public good. To recognise this incurs the risk of stepping outside of the dominant ideology, and therefore of being redefined as 'unprofessional', 'unscientific', 'irresponsible', 'unethical', etc. It is not therefore only psychologists' labour that is the property of dominant institutions, it may also be their very mentality, including psychology itself. Again, this is not to slight psychologists: they do not differ in this respect from a host of other groups in society.

The report of a working party of the British Psychological Society (McEwen, 1978) may illustrate the over-riding force of dominant assumptions where practical ethical problems arise. The working party's terms of reference had been to invite evidence on the abuse of psychology for political purposes and to make recommendations for appropriate action on the part of the Society. 'Early in its discussions, it was plain to members of the working party that it was necessary to interpret these terms of reference strictly and to set limits upon the range of issues considered': why or how, it was not considered necessary to reveal. A main stimulus to establishing the working party in the first place had been the concern of some members of the Society about the use of 'psychological methods' of interrogation by security forces in Northern Ireland. The working party stated that the KGB had used such methods first, and anyway their use in Northern Ireland had now ceased: even so 'it is right that we, as psychologists, should show some concern that such methods might be used again and elsewhere'. The working party further considered that circumstances which, however deplorable in themselves, did not involve psychological science or practice (an interesting distinction!) lay outside of its remit, and that it had neither time nor resources to investigate alleged abuses abroad. It did, however, make a firm exception to both these principles:

> . . . the use in the Soviet Union of mental hospitals as psychiatric prisons for the detention of human rights activists and other sane people . . . while strictly this involves psychiatry rather than psychology, we feel it appropriate that the Society should join with the Royal College of Psychiatrists in protests on this matter.

Psychological techniques — of whatever kind (Suedefield, 1979) — may or may not be in current use by our own state authorities (Comain, 1978); Soviet pathopsychologists may or may not be involved in the enforced psychiatric treatment of people who disagree with the way in which their society is run, in a way that clinical and educational psychologists in this country could surely never be (but then who has checked this point for either country?); British psychiatrists may or may not be involved in giving involuntary treatment to people who are 'sane' (perhaps an odd concept for psychologists to use). But the working party knew where lies right and where lies wrong, and where corporate action ought to be directed. Any other action, the working party made it clear, was up to individual members. This is not to impugn the honour of the working party, they merely stated what they thought was right. One must, however, question the origin of the concept of 'right' suggested by their reasoning and choice of target, and most of all their immediate assumption that the only moral dispute that could properly arise about 'political abuse' is a judgemental one within a single way of thinking so self-evident as to require neither definition nor justification. Moral disputes may also be criterial, involving the conflicting claims of separate moral codes that present rival concepts of what constitute 'abuse' and 'political purposes'.

The British Psychological Society only admits graduates of recognised courses, a consideration that might have excluded a number of some of the major innovative figures in psychological science. Its internal structure reflects the institutions that employ us, rather than 'scientific' categories. Within the BPS there are 'scientific affairs' and 'professional affairs' (the latter, note, nothing to do with trade unionism), reflecting the general separation of 'academic' psychologists from those who practise in the real world. Practitioners divide themselves in ways that reflect their workplaces: thus the Division of Clinical Psychology represents the centralised and standardised operation of a national health service, with its strict and formalised criteria for admission to professional status; the Division of Educational and Child Psychology represents the more amorphous shape of local government, with its relatively open door for those who care to work in that field. As the divisions and differentiations in employment increase, so too do the divisions and differentiations in our own apparently independent professional groupings multiply to match them. Within local government a promotion structure has been established for psychological practitioners, with promotion of course largely in the hands of the employer and not necessarily dependent upon merit or skill as a psychologist. Now a separate body has been established to represent the interests and views of 'chiefs' in local authority educational psychology. Were such a body ever to be in a position to 'represent' psychology to central or local government organisations then the direct control of psychology at the workplace, and the more general ideological organisation of psychological practice according to a particular view of what psychology ought to be, would have converged.

Ingleby (1975) has suggested that one should not expect to liberate child psychology 'by intellectual thoroughness alone, but by withdrawal of one's allegiance to the interest groups defended by the present framework'. He concluded

> . . . it is not enough simply to set off in pursuit of a wider range of viewpoints — as if by some ingenious system of mirrors one would see what the world would look like from a different position in the political order: one doesn't escape so easily from the bemusement of one's own mentality, from the habits of thought and perception laid down in the many years spent socialising into a class or a profession. The only way to analyse just what this mentality is, and the shortest route to an understanding of it . . . is by discovering the power structure that props it up.

As has been argued above, however, 'withdrawal of one's allegiance' may put the psychologist at risk of unemployment. How might psychologists both increase awareness of the situation in which they and their psychology are placed and, most importantly, do something positive about it, without achieving no more than personal hardship for themselves and their dependants. Most important of all, how might psychologists contribute to diversifying psychological practice, breaking away from the psychological monoculture that predominates in our major state institutions, to provide the diversity of psychological theory and practice that our society might need in its own rapidly changing circumstances?

There seems no readily apparent solution to be found of continuing on the course presently pursued by local authority psychologists as a group. With a few notable personal exceptions this large body of psychologists seems to be sinking lower and lower within the institutions of which they are a part, and whatever insights this might provide into the experience of the oppressed it does not do much to enable them to operate as agents for change. Moreover, the focus of their work, whatever its realities, seems increasingly to be perceived in official and public eyes as a service dealing with the most inconvenient of society's casualties. Such a perception carries not only the short-term danger of having the 'pressing needs' of such cases take precedence over all other work, it bears also the risk of redefining psychologists as a sort of para-welfare profession, whose responsibilities, numbers, etc. should be determined by the incidence, 'needs', etc. of the maladjusted and the failing rather than by possible contributions to the system as a whole. There is no immediately apparent alternative workplace, other than *via* the local authorities, that is, funded directly by the state. For whatever reasons, the only obvious possibility in this respect, the professional training courses at the universities, have almost universally failed to provide alternative or original practice, original research or practical work of the sort that is not really possible for most psychologists 'in the system' (advocacy for individuals or for causes, for example) – so much so that perhaps the training courses might for the most part be more appropriately placed in the local authorities' own polytechnics than at universities. Raven (e.g. 1975) has argued most convincingly for independent, public funded research institutions, working on a freelance research and development model at the many vital fringes of our practical knowledge, and Sutton (1978a) has proposed a somewhat similar arrangement for directly funded independent practice as a means for stimulating scientific progress. Pleasant dreams . . . but ones with very little likelihood of realisation.

The human concerns with which local authority psychologists could potentially work are areas of legitimate involvement, and this is work which appears most properly conducted as a public institution. At the moment, however, it appears unlikely that local authority psychologists are so placed as to be able to make responses to these concerns beyond a certain and perhaps contracting range determined by the circumstances of their employment, and it may be that these restraints are not altogether to the public good as many would define it. Perhaps paradoxically, therefore, some psychologists might legitimately seek to advance their concerns by creating alternative employment structures outside the present local authority system, by conducting natural experiments with the patronage of psychological practice.

Such a resolution to the long-standing practical and ethical dilemmas within the public practice may be the more realistic for fitting in with the needs of the 'profession' to diversify at a time of economic restraint. The following suggestions for alternative patronage derive from present circumstances: more may emerge if more are forced to re-consider the attractions or the likelihood of work in the established system.

Ladies and Gentlemen, not Players.   There is almost certainly going to be graduate unemployment, at least amongst educational psychologists, and with the traditional safety net of a return to teaching removed there may be no option for some but to go on the dole. What better unparalleled opportunity for practising psychology amongst the needy than being one of them? More experienced practitioners may also find themselves out of work, as a result of limited or enforced geographical movement for family reasons or as a result of parenthood (mainly of course women, in both categories). Whatever the reason for their unemployment, there may well be some who wish to continue to practise in some way, even if there is no money to be made from it. But the vision of out-of-work psychologists' continuing to work, independently and for free, their work supported indirectly by the state by means of unemployment benefit, or dependent upon the lucky chance of a solvent spouse or cohabitee, is probably a romantic one granted mainly to those actually in employment themselves. Psychological practice could be an expensive hobby, and though the psychologist of independent means might be in a very favourable position in certain respects, it would need exceptionally enthusiastic individuals or groups to pursue such a course in favour of more pressing personal necessities and causes.

Other Trades.   One step open to the disillusioned or unemployed psychologist is to abandon the professions for which (s)he has been specifically trained, and seek employment in the real world on the basis of personal merit. The educational psychologist might consider going into a job where the specific training in child-oriented psychology might be put to the test. The cruellest testing ground, the classroom, might be difficult to arrange now, but the psychologist could try exercising the insights of professional training in, say, untrained social work or residential child care. More generally there is a host of jobs in the public service where a postgraduate training in psychology might make a useful contribution to client-welfare, and the experience of which would provide enormous material for psychological investigation. Here, too, it is being suggested that psychology might find a way of drawing continuing sustenence indirectly from the state, in this case surreptitiously fulfilling a public role that obscures the underlying purpose. By far the most notable protagonist of this survival strategy was A. R. Luriya, whose very life perhaps depended upon his apparently giving up psychology altogether for 15 years or so and becoming a physician (see Luriya, 1979). In fact he never ceased to be a psychologist, and his two careers synthesised to create his neuro-psychology and aphasiology. Again, however, it is perhaps rather much to expect all but the most devoted enthusiast, in advantageous circumstances, to be able to maintian a dual identity in the new workplace to a degree sufficient to achieve any level of synthesis.

Private Practice.   What little full-time private psychological practice
there has been so far in this country appears to have been conducted
largely in the London area. The extremely small size of our private
sector has doubtless in part been a function of the high cost of
providing a psychological service, and doubtless in part a function of the
non-commercial backgrounds of most practising psychologists. In part,
too, it may have reflected the general availability of free public
services *somewhere*, as long as the potential client persisted in trying to
find them. But though local authority psychologists are now relatively
plentiful in most parts of the country it can often be difficult for
people with 'middle-class' problems to attract the sort of attention
that they feel themselves to deserve. At the same time the relative cost
of the psychologists' time has dropped in terms of the earning power
of many other groups. For example, in the sixties a miner or an army
sergeant could hardly have conceived of buying such services. In the
eighties the continuing erosion of differentials makes a much wider
clientele possible, and a market might open up for private practice that
can afford to look around for better answers than 'placement in a
secondary school with a good remedial department'. Parents who are
not amongst the least well-off groups in our society might well be
willing to devote their surplus wealth to finding personal and effective
help about, for example, an apparently normal child who unaccount-
ably fails to learn at school, or a young handicapped child who lacks
basic social skills, rather than rely on routinised and perhaps
ineffective provisions within the state system. Those whose social
consciences are offended by such private trading might reflect that the
harsh economics of such a market-place could introduce a degree of
direct accountability and reality-testing that is not apparent in the
general run of public practice, and that the demands engendered might
prove a useful spur for psychological practice as a whole.

The Courts.   A wing of private contracting barely explored in this
country to date involves work for clients who are involved in legal
proceedings (in distinction to 'court work' within local authority
assessment procedures for juveniles). Some American psychologists
have used the courts as an important means of stimulating social change
(not least for other American psychologists), and though their legal and
constitutional situation differs from ours in many respects our own
courts are much closer to the centres of public debate than are the
recesses of local government. Court cases involving children, whatever
the issue (offending, offended against or disputed over), now lean

heavily upon 'expert' evidence on child development, behaviour and adult–child interactions, and depend upon 'the professionals' for many of their disposals: as much of this professional expertise is both 'psychological' and suspect, there is great scope for a real forensic-science contribution. A considerable proportion of such work might be financed indirectly by the state, this time *via* Legal Aid, in a way that offers the psychologist a professional autonomy of a kind analogous to that of the lawyers with whom (s)he would be dealing (see Fielding and Portwood, 1980). It offers the possibility of examining some very basic issues, in a context where they have to bear the brunt not only of the adversary system but also of public scrutiny. It also offers an arena in which public exposure is accompanied by a high degree of personal protection, where the psychologist who has a strong case to make out can do so relatively free from immediate institutional reprisal.

'Consultancy Work'.   This term appears already to have attached to private contracting to institutions rather than to individuals. There have long been independent institutions that pay psychologists fees or retainers for their services, for example voluntary bodies and their schools, training boards and the Open University. In the latter case, again, the state is paying indirectly. There is an enormously wider range of institutions that feel free to comment upon matters relating to, say, education, child care and family welfare. If for example the TUC or the CBI consider it important that they should have policies about pre-school provision or educational standards, then perhaps some enterprising psychologist could sell them the idea that they could perhaps do more than just opine themselves, or survey the opinions of their members. The psychological practices generated by such bodies might differ substantially from that of the official bodies, the LEAs, the Schools Council or the NFER: it would be interesting to see too how they differed one from the other. Paid consultancy need not of course be solely for large bodies: there are local, community-based organisations closely involved in problems of childhood, and small pressure groups addressing specific areas of policy. They too might have require-ments that a psychologist would fulfil – though they might not be able to pay as well.

Supra-national Patronage.   The above suggestions all involve alterna-tives to state patronage that are provided for us within the state itself, by virtue of its pluralistic nature. It is possible, however, that patronages exist for psychologists outside of the gentle tolerance of our own immediate society. The EEC has moneys to spend on matters that are the legitimate concern of psychologists, it also has power to establish regulations in areas of concern that might overlap with some psychologists' practice. The obvious analogy with federal funding and federal laws is not a direct one at the present level of development of the European Community, but when one considers the enormous freedoms that have been granted to American psychologists (and others) by federal 'programs', it is hard to resist the hope that similar remarkable opportunities might be created for ourselves in some foreseeable future.

To express reservations about the virtual monopoly of psychological practice presently held by major state institutions in this country should not imply consideration of some form of institutional determinism. We all know local authority psychologists who 'get away with murder' at work, despite or unbeknown to their employers. They often regard such activity as the high points of their work, but it necessarily remains underground, a psychological black economy. Perhaps this in part explains why educational psychologists as a group contribute so little of their achievement to the public domain (Hart and Taylor, 1979). A notable exception is to be found in the well-publicised work of Loxley and his colleagues in Sheffield (e.g. Loxley, 1978), who have sought to create a form of 'community psychology' under the auspices of a generally sympathetic and progressive local authority. Discussing the leading role that a Sheffield psychologist played in the widely publicised 'child sterilisation case' (still the only documented case of child advocacy by a local authority psychologist), Loxley (1976) was at pains to emphasise their reliance upon the licence of an (on balance) benevolent authority.

> In the case in question the child's rights would have been effectively abrogated by the decision of the doctors and the mother, had they not been persistently defended by the psychologist. The head teacher and social worker involved, although supporting the psychologist, had been quietly advised by their union and supervisor respectively not to pursue the matter. There being no institutional obligation on the Education Authority to defend the child's rights, the psychologist felt obliged to take a personal stand, and possibly a professional risk. Since there is no 'Children's Ombudsman' it meant turning to the courts and the glare of publicity as the case became a *cause célèbre*.
>
> In many local authorities the initiative taken by the psychologist

in this case would have been regarded as outside, and possibly in breach of her contract. The situation could have been that whereas the Health Service administration confessed itself powerless to intervene in the 'clinical freedom' of a doctor, the local authority *might* have claimed the right to restrain the professional freedom of its psychologist . . .

Institutional bureaucracies are hide-bound by precedents, and even when the buck-passing stops between subordinate and superior, in the end a division of opinion amongst the elected representatives could be enough to curtail more than a gesture of concern. Also there is the question of the future relationships between an organisation, such as local authority Education Department or Social Services Department, and (in this case) the local personnel of the Health Service. Organisations prefer compromise to open conflict and individual workers are sometimes regarded as more expendable than institutional relationships.

In the event the divided councillors did manage to muster a majority statement of support for their psychologist at the request of senior officers. Had the Authority been asked to commit itself to direct legal action it seems probable that the outcome would have been a different story. This was a case where personal and professional ethics, the client's and the public interest were weighed in the balance. In the end there was no time for strict protocol and the decision to 'go it alone' took courage, as the judge later observed.

Loxley's account should act as a reminder that neither generally nor in specific cases should 'the state' be reified as some monolithic, omni-compitant and malevolent entity. It and its institutions consist of groups and individuals with conflicting self-interests. But if it 'took courage' for the psychologist to act in what she saw as the only way ethically open to her, even where the employing authority was in the main sympathetic and supportive, then we have to accept that, whatever attributes and aspirations local authority psychologists may hold *as people*, the general tenor of their practice will be 'conservative' (Ingleby, 1975), and 'act to support the *status quo*' (Durndell, 1977). Moreover, we have to accept that whatever alternative patronage might be sought out by some psychologists, the bulk of psychological practice, and its costly training programme, will remain firmly in the hands of the state.

Perhaps concern over this is quite superfluous. Perhaps the *status quo* is the best of all possible worlds, and the outcome of our labours is indeed expressed solely in insights and techniques that improve the quality of life of our fellow citizens. Perhaps our masters both recognise and accept that what we do leads inevitably to other people's having to change or even give up what they do, that innovation from ourselves leads to obsolescence in others. Perhaps people are happy to recognise that one product of psychological advances might be new ways of thinking about human affairs, and that one area of the obsolescence that we might create might involve their own cherished ideas of what is 'right', 'natural', etc. Perhaps therefore the public institutions for which we work will of their own accord establish means whereby we (amongst others) may generate, explore and evaluate new ways of ensuring the welfare that they are mandated to provide. Probably they will not. It is more likely that the circumstances in which we work, together with our present public services, will (without the need to suggest any conscious 'conspiracy') combine to direct much of our efforts towards other outcomes.

When psychological practice was younger, its technical tools were largely 'passive' at the level of our own practice, indeed the local authority psychologist often produced little more than measurements. In the hands of others, however, even these (to us) passive tools provided powerful means of social control. Increasingly, however, our own professional aspirations push our practice towards more active skills, initially the effective change of others' behaviour and now the efficient organisation of whole groups. We have already begun to struggle (admittedly with little success as yet) with the 'last frontier' of psychology within our present vision, the conscious manipulation of the mechanisms determining development itself. Psychological practice is beginning to sense powerful new abilities almost within its grasp. When it is able to exercise them, psychologists (like many other scientists before them) might wish that they had paid more attention earlier on to what they were doing, and whom they were doing it for. And so might everyone else.

Appendix

The *Decision of the Industrial Tribunal* (1978) referred to in this chapter is of particular relevance to psychologists practising for local authorities, though there is no immediate reason to feel that psychologists practising in other fields might be wholly free from its implications. The Tribunal sat on thirteen occasions between March and

October 1978, but its deliberations and findings were not reported in the *Bulletin of the British Psychological Society*, the *Occasional Papers of the Division of Educational and Child Psychology* or the *Journal of the Association of Educational Psychologists*. Few psychologists heard more than vague rumours, and there must be many who have not heard of it at all.

The applicant had been appointed as an educational psychologist by the County Borough of Reading in April 1972. Following the Local Government Act (1972) the educational functions of Reading Borough Council (including its educational psychologists) were transferred to Berkshire County Council, with effect from 1 April 1974. The applicant was dismissed from the service of Berkshire County Council on 3 June 1977 with immediate effect, for gross misconduct. The Tribunal was held in response to his claim of unfair dismissal. The case proved a complex one, and both applicant and respondent were criticised by the Tribunal. It is not, however, the specific rights and wrongs of this case that are of general interest, but a more general point that the Tribunal itself made central to its subsequent decision.

The charge of 'gross misconduct' had involved a number of counts. The Tribunal was clear about what constituted the principal reason for dismissal amongst those cited by the County Council.

It is the Tribunal's finding that the principal reason for dismissal was the applicant's conduct in the handling of cases ... The Tribunal is fully satisfied that the applicant's persistant refusal to conform to his employer's instructions in this matter for example by failing to conduct and record tests and by evading investigation of such cases as were the cause of complaint, was sufficient reason to justify his dismissal on 3 June 1977. (para. 38)

Contributory to this finding were the Tribunal's views on certain aspects of what psychologists might regard as their 'professionalism'.

It is appropriate, at this stage, to state that the (applicant's) 'philosophical reasons' for ignoring the instructions of the respondent Council in the matter of examination and assessment of children were at the heart of the problem which later arose in a number of specific cases of which the respondent Council was complaining. Throughout the hearing, the applicant's case was founded on the concept that he was in some way an independent professional consultant who had children referred to him as 'clients'.

Even accepting that it was common parlance for children dealt with
by educational psychologists to be referred to as 'clients', the
Tribunal could not accept that the applicant was in any way acting
other than as an employee to whom instructions could properly be
given on the policy to be followed in the treatment of cases for
which the respondent Council was responsible. The point was also
made on behalf of the applicant that notes and correspondence
written by him in relation to cases for which the respondent Council
was responsible were confidential to him and, therefore, his own
private porperty ... The Tribunal was unable to accept his view; the
children were referred to the applicant in the exercise of the
respondent Council's responsibility for the educational needs of the
children, the applicant was an employee engaged to deal with such
cases in the course of his duties and the notes and correspondence
about them, prepared by him in the course of carrying out these
duties, were clearly part of the respondent Council's records and
available to it at all times ...

The Tribunal heard further evidence from 2 highly qualified
psychologists from other local education authorities on the merits
or otherwise of carrying out intelligence tests and the value of
working to the Manual on the Wechsler Intelligence Test for
Children. The views expressed by these experts were at variance on
this precise issue but the fundamental point remained that, whereas
in some local education authorities, the need for and value of
intelligence tests might be virtually disregarded, in others an entirely
different view is taken. The Director of Education of the respondent
Council was responsible to his authority for the placement of
children and he, from the outset when the applicant was transferred
to the respondent Council's service, had made it clear, on behalf of
his authority, that he required examination and assessment to be
carried out and to be the subject of written reports. The Tribunal
was unable to accept the applicant's contention that, because he
held different views about the assessment and testing of children, he
was at liberty to ignore instructions given on behalf of the respondent Council on its requirements for the treatment of cases for which
it, as an education authority, bore responsibility. (paras. 17–18)

The Tribunal reached the unanimous decision that the applicant had
not been unfairly dismissed.

In the context of the present discussion it matters not what other
factors were involved in the applicant's dismissal or the Tribunal's

decision, nor the particular professional qualification of the applicant. The Tribunal raised important questions of principle that transcend this specific case and potentially apply to *all* psychological practice. In reaching its decision the Tribunal had mind of the precedents of a number of previous cases, that did not involve psychologists, and created a further one that did.

10 PSYCHOLOGICAL PRACTICE IN A SOCIAL CONTEXT

Andrew Sutton and Ian McPherson

Over the last decade we have been urged to 'reconstruct' educational research (Shulman, 1970), social psychology (Armistead, 1974) and educational psychology (Gillham, 1978). But the seventies were largely a time of building rather than reconstruction and there was growth rather than change. Now, however, psychologists along with everyone else are coming to accept that the days of expansion are over, and to question the implication of this for psychological practice.

Psychological practice now involves greater numbers than ever before, comprising people of a different kind than a generation ago, with new approaches and wider aspirations, but psychology itself is still structured in the old forms. Inevitably, therefore, its institutions are subject to conflict and stress. At a theoretical level there is tension between the 'new' schools and the 'old' that co-exist with increasing difficulty within a supposedly unitary 'psychology'. Among psychologists themselves there are continuing artificial distinctions made between research and practice ('academic' and 'professional'), institutionalised within the British Psychological Society in the Boards and the Sections and Divisions. There is the separation of clinical and educational psychology, which depends more upon the requirements of employment than on any specifically 'psychological' considerations. There is a system of professional training, initially set up on an *ad hoc* basis to create a relatively low grade of psychological operative for the health or education service from a pool of people with first degrees in psychology, now trying to match vastly expanded professional aspirations within the confines of still relatively short pre-experience courses. There is the 'clogging' of promotional ladders that were filled almost as soon as they were created in a period of rapid expansion, curtailing any substantial promotion prospects for nearly all newer entrants for years to come. There is a disparity between many employers' expectations of what psychologists should do and the psychologists' own aspirations. There is a growing recognition that clients have aspirations too, and that much previous practice may have offended rather than realised these.

Psychology, of course, has always been in a state of flux. New approaches emerge, old styles of working drop out of fashion, and there are always psychologists who are different or dissatisfied. Variability in practice has been commonplace in public service pshcyology, and so too have been the small personal stresses as individuals conflict with their fellows, their clients or their employers, over precisely what they are trying to achieve and the ways in which they set out to do it. But the minor tensions of recent years have been largely contained by expansion, negotiation and minor adjustment, and advances have been incorporated in an evolutionary way. Common concerns and formulations have coalesced into discernible movements which have met with the often grudging acknowledgement of those not directly involved. Thus the last ten years have seen psychometric measurement abandoned as the essential practical tool of the practising psychologist, and the emergence of 'therapies', 'treatments', 'interventions' etc. as core skills for psychologists making a direct provision to clients and client groups. But though such shifts in practice have been far reaching in many respects, they have had no fundamental effects upon the overall model in which psychological practice is generally conceived. Psychology in the NHS and the local authorities has remained primarily one of the 'helping' or 'people' professions, and dissatisfaction within psychology at this 'clinical' role has been relatively easily absorbed into the larger whole over the course of the massive expansion during the seventies. Now, however, economic recession is producing a new stress upon this system that cannot be eased by such means. The period of major growth is over, the employment market may, at best, hold steady and may even contract. The changing economic balance of power and the advent of new technologies are transforming the whole pattern of wealth and employment in the world, with this country (especially its less advantaged citizens) likely to make a net loss from the changeover. If the whole social context in which our psychology is employed undergoes a corresponding shift it seems highly unlikely that minor adjustments within psychology will remain sufficient to maintain our practice in equilibrium with its rapidly changing environment. Already the large number of psychologists currently employed find themselves increasingly in competition for jobs in the old hegemonies. Educational psychologists want to work in the NHS; clinical psychologists in the local authorities. The Virgin Lands in the social services departments, the penal system and 'the community' are being eagerly explored by psychologists of all kinds. Psychologists are becoming uncomfortably (or in some cases eagerly) aware that their professional future can no longer be conceived of as just an extension of the present. Old aspirations, however firmly held, old ways of working, however enjoyed or appreciated, old achievements, however hard won, must now come under critical review. It may be that tensions both within psychology itself, and between psychology and those outside, mean that conflict rather than consensus will be the mark of our immediate future: if we are at last forced to produce something other than more of the same, then evolution will have to give way to revolution in psychological practice.

A social practice

Within British psychology today there are a number of possible alternatives to present practice, with protagonists eager for wider acceptance. The theme that runs through the contributions to this book is that there should be a change in the level at which psychological investigation and intervention should be directed. The dominant model that is now 'traditional' in the professional practice of psychology has focused upon the individual, with at most an acknowledgement of immediate environmental constraints, reinforcers etc. To many the word 'psychological' has come to imply phenomena largely coterminous with the individual client, and 'psychological explanations' and 'psychologisation' have become perjorative terms to indicate a narrow, even reactionary, reductionist interpretation of human affairs. In contrast, our contributors have emphasised the need to broaden the scope of psychology by moving away from what is happening 'within' the individual and his immediate environment, and raising the attention to incorporate how individuals are affected by organisations and social systems. Psychological practice is thus to be reconstructed by analysing and influencing the ways in which these wider phenomena function, as an essential component of any dealings with the individuals within them. This approach is advanced as a more efficient and effective means of serving not only already existing client groups but also groups with whom the present model allows little or no practice. Psychological practice in the public sector, they suggest, is to be more of a social psychology than hitherto, and in making this suggestion some of them turn (paradoxically, it may appear) to the private sector of organisational and industrial psychology for their conceptual tools.

If it does turn out that the social and organisational approach proves in keeping with the spirit and economic realities of the time, then in retrospect it will appear that the new stage is already well under way in established departures and innovations in practice, many as yet undocumented. In anticipation one ought to consider some of the possible implications of this approach both for psychologists and their psychology.

The Knowledge Base. The core areas of knowledge proper to psychologists, experimental method, learning theory, etc. will presumably remain largely unchanged, but they will be exercised in a vastly extended context. Specific professional knowledge has drawn heavily in the past from 'intra-personal' areas of knowledge, such as linguistics, physiology and medicine, incorporating not just their data but often their models too. In future the practising psychologists may often need knowledge from 'extra-personal' or social areas, such as organisational, environmental and social psychology, sociology, politics and economics, again, with different models as well as data. Psychologists will still be concerned with individual development, behaviour, learning, psychopathology, etc., but will need to understand them as aspects of a wider social whole and to direct their attempts to intervene in ways that include mechanisms operating at both the micro- and the macro-level. Psychologists may find in doing so that the mechanisms that *link* these two levels are as yet barely known.

Professional Contacts. Our principle professional contacts (whether we would have wished it or not) have to date been from the ranks of the 'multi-disciplinary team', with other 'helping professionals' such as teachers, doctors, social workers, nurses, etc. True, psychologists who have been promoted up through the ranks that psychology now has in its various public service manifestations have found themselves in contact with managers and bureaucrats, even with elected representatives, but their role in that context has been largely to act as experienced (or at least ex-) practitioners, rather than as technical experts at this new level of work in its own right. If the knowledge base of psychological practice expands then the nature of our professional contacts, even amongst the most junior members of the profession, will expand correspondingly, and psychologists will seek membership of new 'teams', including social administrators, planners and politicians, not merely as a representative of a 'lower-order' discipline but as essential contributors in their own right to any decisions intended to influence individual behaviour.

Client Contacts. This approach explicitly denies the possibility and the credibility of a direct personal contact by the psychologist with *all* the clients whom it might benefit. It also implies that the psychologist's client-centred work should be conducted with some wider social purpose than solely to help that one individual. It does not cut psychologists off from individual clients as an essential focus of psychological practice, rather it presents the opportunities, dilemmas and dangers, both to psychologists and their employers, of a deliberate choice of client groups, a deliberate discrimination for the sake of some and against the interests of others. None of this is of course new, but if the analysis of social issues is incorporated into the psychologist's technical expertise then the choices made on behalf of clients will be exercised differently, and a different set of priorities might emerge.

Training. Postgraduate training courses in clinical and educational psychology already find it hard to cover the range of knowledge and skills regarded desirable for current practice. It seems unlikely that we will have resources to extend training substantially in the foreseeable future. The post-qualification training courses already suggested in both clinical and educational psychology have been made primarily in response to the perceived limitations of pre-qualification training in meeting existing demands. The training courses must of course cater for existing needs, but they surely have an obligation, too, to offer a lead to psychologists working in the field (as many did in the switch from psychometrics to intervention in the seventies). What then should be their priorities? How could they incorporate, even with the help of post-experience or 'refresher' courses, the vast, unfamiliar mass of knowledge represented by the bibliography to the present volume? There may be no satisfactory answers to these questions, and the present system of three years of undergraduate psychology plus one or two years postgraduate training could be one of the structures of professional practice that will also have to change. It may be more effective, for example, rather than looking to extending professional training 'up' into further postgraduate work, to look instead to extending it 'down' into the present undergraduate years, by means of a more vocationally oriented first degree in psychology.

The Psychologists. People come into psychological practice for an infinity of reasons, and this is unlikely to change. But the orientation of this calling to 'helping' individuals, rather than to more broadly-based social interpretations of the human condition, has certainly brought a skew to the distribution. One might predict that a more social and organisational orientation to psychological practice would attract more entrants with different personal and social goals.

Psychology might, much more than has been the case in recent years, attract recruits who see it as a way into a career in managing and organising our social institutions, or conversely as a means for radical, social action. In either case political considerations may be more explicitly expressed in their work than has been a feature of psychological practice in this country.

The Work.   In addition to the interpersonal skills relevant to working with clients the psychologist who wishes to be involved in intervention at decision-making levels will have to learn skills of negotiation and confrontation. Whatever activities are appropriate at the 'helping' level, psychologists will have to operate with conflict as a feature of their work (though not necessarily, of course, the predominant one). A more social approach to psychological practice brings immediate conflict with the 'old school' of practitioners, some of whom find the new style of working anathemous and a rejection of the fruits of their own hard-won victories. It brings conflict too with 'colleagues' in the other helping professions, some of whom have had trouble enough accepting the psychologist as a partner in their 'teams', and few of whom are able to accept the additional change to becoming the psychologists' subjects in their own right. It promises further conflict with many of those already in 'advisory' or 'managerial' positions (especially perhaps in local government): if the psychologist does indeed have expertise of this level, then it is often advanced at the expense of the ignorance of others. Many areas of psychological practice demand great personal skill as well as technical knowledge for their successful implementation: a broadening of the technical knowledge base might demand even wider personal skills.

The Psychology.   The contributors to this volume have advanced suggestions about psychological practice that represent an indigenous response to our indigenous problems. They have concentrated on the direction of psychological practice and the means whereby it might be structured, but not on the psychology itself. If indeed changes such as they advocate lead to a new pattern of psychological practice in this country, then over the next decade psychology will find itself operating in new arenas, in different company and with different models, and it will include those with unfamiliar backgrounds and outlooks. Perhaps it is not too much to hope that a new body of psychological theory will arise from within psychological practice, incorporating the many influences and gains from psychology 'outside', from academic psychology, from psychology in the private sector, and psychology abroad, but providing its own synthesis directly dependent upon the personal and social realities of the clients and the institutions that work with them.

Plus Ça Change . . .

To suggest that psychologists should now direct their attention beyond the individual level is not a rejection of previous work, but a progression from it. To continue to work solely with individuals would certainly be easier and less threatening for psychologists; it might even be more likely, in the short term at least, to improve their 'professional standing'. It would also, however, be an admission of psychologists' lack of interest in influencing factors of major importance in people's lives, and hence confirmation of the suspicion of many that whatever psychology is about it is nothing to do with them. Whatever changes are brought about in the practice of psychology, by forces within it or without, whatever advances occur in psychological knowledge, there will doubtless remain many psychologists who will go on acting in the old ways, because both they and those with whom they work are happiest if they continue to do so. And even discounting survivals from present-day practice, it seems highly likely that certain important features of psychological practice in this country will remain largely unchanged, whatever happens short of total catastrophy. Psychological practice will still be conducted overwhelmingly within the public service, paid for mainly by the National Health Service and local authorities; it will provide an attractive career, relatively secure and well paid, and increasingly competitive at the point of entry; it will remain 'professional' in its aspirations, a 'conspiracy against the laity' as well as an altruistic attempt to bring science to the service of suffering humanity. Whatever the innovations of psychological theory and practice, the major problems to which psychologists direct their efforts in the public service, the affairs of the poor, pupils, patients and prisoners, may very well remain largely unmitigated. Indeed, despite all out efforts, they may even get worse! For all the changes discussed in this book, certain things may remain very much the same.

This is one other constant to be discerned amongst the chapters of this book. There is no single psychological viewpoint, and the common features advanced by the contributors are matched by disagreements about precisely how these features might best be exercised for the common good. If the broader social approach advocated here does indeed prove a dominant model for psychological practice in this country, then there is already within it ample scope for future dissatisfaction and dissention, and ultimately presumably for some yet more distant reconstruction beyond our present powers to foresee.

BIBLIOGRAPHY

Acklaw, J. 1979. Educational psychology: am I deluded? *Bulletin of the British Psychological Society*, **32**, 283–4.

Adams, S. 1967. A cost approach to the assessment of gang rehabilitation techniques. *Journal of Research in Crime and Delinquency*, **4**, 166–82.

Agras, W. S., Sylvester, D. and Oliveau, D. C. 1969. The epidemiology of common fears and phobias. *Comprehensive Psychiatry*, **10**, 151–6.

Ainscow, M., Bond, J., Gardner, J. and Tweddle, D. 1978. The development of a three-part evaluation procedure for inset courses. *British Journal of In-Service Education*, **4**, 184–90.

Ainscow, M. and Tweddle, D. 1977. Behavioural objectives and children with learning difficulties. *Journal of the Association of Educational Psycholoigsts*, **4**(5), 29–32.

Ainscow, M. and Tweddle, D. A. 1979. *Preventing Classroom Failure.* London: Wiley.

Albee, G. W. 1959. *Mental Health Manpower Trends.* New York: Basic Books.

Albee, S. W. 1968. Conceptual models and manpower requirements in psychology. *American Psychologist*, **23**, 317–20.

Alexander, F. and Healy, W. 1935. *Roots of Crime.* New York: Knopf.

Allen, P. 1979. The role of the psychologist in the Social Services. In P. Williams (ed.) *Proc. Conf. on the Role of the Psychologist in Soc. Services.* Wallingford, Oxon, Castle Priory College.

Allen, P. 1980. What can the psychologist offer SSDs? *Community Care*, 17 January, 26–7.

Anderson, S. and Hasler, J. C. 1979. Counselling in general practice. *Journal of the Royal College of General Practitioners*, **29**, 352–7.

Arends, R. I. and Arends, J. H. 1977. *Systems Change Strategies in Educational Settings.* London: Human Science Press.

Armistead, N. (ed.) 1974. *Reconstructing Social Psychology.* London: Penguin.

Asher, M. A. 1970. The attainments of children in ESN schools and remedial departments. *Educational Research*, **12**, 215–19.

Association of Educational Psychologists. 1976. *Psychological Services for Local Authorities* (Revised edn). Durham: AEP.

Ayllon, T. 1975. Behaviour modification in institutional settings.

Arizona Law Review, 17, 3–19.

Baher, E., Hyman, C., Jones, R., Kerr, A. and Mitchell, R. 1976. *At Risk: an Account of the Work of the Battered Child Research Department.* London: Routledge and Kegan Paul.

Bailey, T. and de Souza, D. 1980. A systematic study of a school for children with severe learning difficulties. Unpublished MEd Thesis. University of Exeter.

Bailey, W. G. 1966. Correctional outcome: an evaluation of 100 reports. *Journal of Criminal Law, Criminology and Police Science*, 57, 153–60.

Bandura, A. 1969. *Principles of Behaviour Modification.* New York: Holt, Rinehart and Winston.

Bandura, A. 1978. On paradigms and recycled ideologies. *Cognitive Research and Therapy*, 2, 79–105.

Barden, J. I. 1977. The state of the art (and science) of school psychology. *American Psychologist*, 31, 785–91.

Barden, V. 1979. Basic data for manpower planning in clinical psychology. *Bulletin of the British Psychological Society*, 32, 12–16.

Becker, W. C. 1977. Teaching reading and language to the disadvantaged: what we have learned from field research. *Harvard Educational Review*, 47, 518–43.

Beishon, J. and Peters, G. 1972. *Systems Behaviour.* London: Harper and Row.

Bender, M. P. 1972. The role of the community psychologist. *Bulletin of the British Psychological Society*, 25, 211–18.

Bender, M. P. 1976. *Community Psychology.* London: Methuen.

Bender, M. P. 1979a. Community psychology — when? *Bulletin of the British Psychological Society*, 32, 6–9.

Bender, M. P. 1979b. Welcome to Newham — gateway to community psychology. In P. Williams (ed.) *Proc. Conf. on the Role of the Psychologist in Social Services.* Wallingford, Oxon, Castle Priory College.

Berg, I., Constantine, M., Hullin, R., McGuire, R. and Tyrer, S. 1978. The effect of two randomly allocated court procedures on truancy. *British Journal of Criminology*, 18, 232–44.

Berg, I., Hullin, R., McGuire, R. and Tyrer, S. 1977. Truancy and the courts: research note. *Journal of Child Psychology and Psychiatry*, 18, 359–65.

Berger, M. 1975. Clinical psychology services for children. *Bulletin of the British Psychological Society*, 28, 102–7.

Beveridge Report (Cmd No. 6404). 1942. *Social Insurance and Allied Services.* London: HMSO.

Bevington, P., Gardner, J. and Cocks, R. 1978. An approach to the planning and evaluation of a parental involvement course. *Child: Care Health and Development*, 4, 217–27.

Bhagat, M., Lewis, A. and Shillitoe, R. 1979. Clinical psychologists and the primary care team. *Update*, February, 479–88.

Bhattacharyya, A. C. 1975. Present roles and practices of local authority educational psychologists and child psychiatrists in child guidance services. Unpublished MEd Dissertation. University of Birmingham: School of Education.

Bitensky, R. 1978. Social work: a non-existent profession in search of itself. *New Universities Q.*, Winter, 65–73.

Braukmann, J. D. and Fixsen, D. L. 1975. Behaviour modification with delinquents. In M. Hersen, R. M. Eisler and P. M. Miller (eds). *Progress in Behaviour Modification*, Vol. 1. New York: Academic Press.

Brindle, P. 1974. The ascertainment of mild subnormality in education. Unpublished MEd Dissertation. University of Birmingham: School of Education.

British Psychological Society. 1973. Report on the role of psychologists in the Health Services. *Bulletin of the British Psychological Society*, 26, 309–30.

British Psychological Society. 1979. *Evidence to the DHSS Joint Working Group on the Primary Health Care Team.* Leicester: BPS.

Broadbent, D. E. 1980. Chronic effects from the physical nature of work. In B. Gardell and G. Johansonn (eds.). *Man and Working Life.* London: J. Wiley.

Broadhurst, A. 1972. Clinical psychology and the general practitioner. *British Medical Journal*, 1, 793–5.

Broadhurst, A. 1977. What part does general practice play in community clinical psychology? *Bulletin of the British Psychological Society*, 30, 305–9.

Brockway, B. 1978. Behavioral medicine in family practice: a unifying approach for the assessment and treatment of psychosocial problems. *Journal of Family Practice*, 6, 545–52.

Brook, A. 1967. An experiment in general practitioner/psychiatrist collaboration. *Journal of the Royal College of General Practitioners*, 13, 127–31.

Brook, A. 1978. An aspect of community mental health: consultative work with general practice teams. *Health Trends*, 10, 37–9.

Brookes, B. 1977. The psychologist in social service assessment centres. *Essex Education*, **31**, 11.

Broome, A. 1978. A psychologist's view of G.P.'s work. In *Psychology and Primary Care: Proceedings of a Joint Meeting of Northern Region and Scottish DCP Branches.* Leicester: BPS.

Brown, B. J. 1977. Gilbey Hone: a token economy management scheme in a residential school for adolescent boys in trouble. *Bulletin of the British Association for Behavioural Psychotherapy*, **5**(3), 79–89.

Brown, B. J. 1978a. Behavioural approaches to child care. *British Journal of Social Work*, **8**, 313–27.

Brown, B. J. 1978b. Preliminary responses to a token economy programme for delinquent boys in a residential school. *Community Home Schools Gazette*, **72**, 96–110.

Brown, B. J. 1979. Towards an expanded role for psychologists in social services departments. In P. Williams (ed.) *Proc. Conf. on the Role of the Psychologist in Social Services*, Wallingford, Oxon, Castle Priory College.

Brown, B. J., Druce, N. R. and Sawyer, C. E. 1978. Individual differences and absconding behaviour, *British Journal of Criminology*, **18**, 62–70.

Brown, B. J. and Sawyer, C. E. 1978. Uses and abuses of psychologists – some alternative for psychologists working in social services departments, *Bulletin British Psychological Society*, **31**, 218–22.

Brown, G. W. and Harris, T. 1978. *Social Origins of Depression: a Study of Psychiatric Disorder in Women.* London: Tavistock.

Bryant, B., Trower, P., Yardley, K., Urbieta, H. and Letemendia, F. J. J. 1976. A survey of social inadequacy amongst psychiatric out patients. *Psychological Medicine*, **6**, 101–12.

Budgett, R. E. B., Morse, S. L. and Stevenson, P. M. 1970. Applying a systems approach in the Royal Navy. In A. J. Romiszowski (ed.). *A Systems Approach to Education and Training* (APLET Occasional Papers No. 1) London: Kogan Page, 34–46.

Burden, R. L. 1978. Schools' systems analysis: a project centred approach. In Gillham, W. (ed.) *Reconstructing Educational Psychology.* London: Croom Helm.

Burden, R. L. 1981. Systems theory and its relevance to schools. In Gillham, W. (ed.) *Problem Behaviour in the Secondary School.* London: Croom Helm.

Burgess, A. 1965. *A Clockwork Orange.* New York: Ballentine.

Burgess, T. 1979. New ways to learn. *Royal Society of Arts Journal.*

Burroughs, G. E. R. 1970. *Design and Analysis in Educational Research.*

Education Monograph, University of Birmingham.

Burt, C. 1925. *The Young Delinquent.* London: ULP.

Caplan, G. 1970. *The Theory and Practice of Mental Health Consultation.* New York: Basic Books.

Cartwright, A. and Anderson, R. 1979. Patients and their doctors, 1977. *Journal of the Royal College of General Practitioners Occasional Paper, 8.*

Channon, L. and Walker, W. 1977. The teaching of psychology in medical schools: A response to Griffiths. *Bulletin of the British Psychological Society*, **30**, 318–19.

Chapman, J. R. 1979. Techniques of economic analysis is psychiatric practice. *British Journal of Medical Psychology*, **52**, 91–7.

Charity Organisation Society. 1870. *Second Annual Report.* London.

Chu, F. and Trotter, S. 1974. *The Madness Establishment: Ralph Nader's Study Group Report on the National Institute of Mental Health.* New York: Grossman.

Clark, D. F. 1979. The clinical psychologist in primary care. *Social Science and Medicine*, **13A**, 707–13.

Clarke, A. D. B. 1978. Predicting human development: problems, evidence, implications. *Bulletin of the British Psychological Society*, **31**, 249–58.

Clarke, A. N. and Clarke, A. D. B. (eds.) 1976. *Early Experience: Myth and Evidence.* London: Open Books.

Clayton, T. 1979. Residential assessment and observation under attack. **5**, 38–41.

Cloward, R. A. and Ohlin, L. E. 1960. *Delinquency and Opportunity: A Theory of Delinquent Gangs.* New York: Free Press.

Cocks, R. P. and Gardner, J. 1979. The role of the educational psychologist in the education of severely subnormal children. *Journal of the Association of Educational Psychologists*, **4(10)**, 13–20.

Cohen, A. K. 1955. *Delinquent Boys: The Culture of the Gang.* Glencoe, Illinois: Free Press.

Cohen, L. 1976. *Educational Research in Classrooms and Schools* London: Harper and Row.

Coleman, J. and Laishley, J. 1977. Expanding the scope of educational psychology. *Child: Care, Health and Development*, **3**, 105–9.

Coleman, J. and Laishley, J. 1978. The psychologist at play. *Community Care*, 1 November, 18–20.

Coleman, J., Rothwell, B. and Watt, C. 1975. Intervention in a day nursery. *Child: Care, Health and Development*, **1**, 413–19.

Comain, L. O. 1978. Abuses of psychology for political purposes (letter). *Bulletin of the British Psychological Society*, **31**, 270.

Cooper, B. 1964. General practitioners' attitudes to psychiatry. *De Medicina Tuenda*, **1**, 43–8.

Cooper, P. 1975. *Social Services Departments' Observation and Assessment Centres for Children.* Birmingham: Movement of Practising Psychologists, Pamphlet No. 3.

Cooper, P. 1976. Why residential assessment? In M. Hughes (ed.) *Observation and Assessment – a Changing Concept.* Birmingham: Selly Oak Colleges, 3–9.

Cooperstock, R. and Lennard, H. L. 1979. Some social meanings of tranquillizer use. *Sociology of Health and Illness*, **1**, 331–45.

Cornish, D. B. and Clarke, R. V. G. 1975. *Residential Treatment and its Effects on Delinquency (Home Office Research Studies No. 32).* London: HMSO.

Corser, C. M. and Ryce, S. W. 1977. Community mental health care: a model based on the primary care team. *British Medical Journal*, **2**, 936–8.

Coupar, A. M. and Kennedy, T. 1980. Running a weight control group: experiences of a psychologist and a general practitioner. *Journal of the Royal College of General Practitioners*, **30**, 41–8.

Cowen, E. L. 1980. The community context. In M. P. Feldman and J. F. Orford (eds.). *Psychological Problems: The Social Context.* London: J. Wiley.

Crane, E. R. 1959. An historical and critical account of the accomplishment quotient idea. *British Journal of Educational Psychology*, **29**, 252–9.

Dalin, P. 1973. *Case Studies of Educational Innovation. IV: Strategies for Innovation in Education.* Centre for Educational Research and Innovation, Organisation for Economic Co-operation and Development.

Davidson, A. F. 1977. Clinical psychology and general practice: a preliminary enquiry. *Bulletin of the British Psychological Society*, **30**, 337–8.

Davidson, A. F. 1979. General practitioner survey on psychological services. Paper presented to London Branch of British Association for Behavioural Psychotherapy.

Davidson, W. S. and Seidman, E. 1974. Studies of behaviour modification and juvenile delinquency: a review, methodological critique and social perspective. *Psychological Bulletin*, **81**, 998–1011.

Department of Education and Science. 1968. *Psychologists in*

Education Services (The Summerfield Report). London: HMSO.

Department of Education and Science. 1975. *The Discovery of Children Requiring Special Education and the Assessment of their Needs* (Circular 2/75). London: HMSO.

Didrichsen, J. 1979. Personally speaking. *Community Care*, 22 February, 14.

Dohrenwend, B. P. and Crandell, D. L. 1970. Psychiatric symptoms in community, clinic and mental hospital groups. *Journal of Psychiatry*, **126**, 1611–21.

Doyle, C. 1980. The dangers of tranquillity. *Observer*, 24 February.

Drewe, E. A. 1971. The fate of Maudsley psychologists. *Bulletin of the British Psychological Society*, **24**, 201–5.

Druce, N. R. 1977. Social learning approaches to professional fostering and treatment within security. In R. M. Jarman *et al.* (eds.). *Behavioural Approaches to the Treatment of Delinquent Adolescents.* Birmingham, Tennal School.

Dunlop, A. B. 1974. *The Approved School Experience (Home Office Research Studies No. 25).* London: HMSO.

Durlak, J. A. 1979. Comparative effectiveness of paraprofessional and professional helpers. *Psychological Bulletin*, **1**, 80–92.

Durndell, A. 1977. Does psychology support the status quo? *Bulletin of the British Psychological Society*, **30**, 320–2.

Earll, L. and Kincey, J. 1980. Evaluation of psychological intervention at primary care level – a controlled trial. Paper presented at the British Psychological Society Annual Conference, Aberdeen.

Eastman, C. and McPherson, I. G. 1980. As others see us: General practitioners' perceptions of psychological problems and the relevance of clinical psychology. In preparation.

Edwardson, B. 1973. The psychologist and social services departments. *DECP Occasional Papers*, Summer, 139–44.

Emery, R. E. and Marholin, D. 1977. An applied behaviour analysis of delinquency: the irrelevancy of relevant behaviour. *American Psychologist*, **6**, 860–73.

Evans, D. and Murray, J. 1969. The improvement of creative thinking abilities of approved schoolboys. *Approved Schools Gaz.*, August, 213–22.

Eysenck, H. J. and Eysenck, S. B. G. 1969. *Personality Structure and Measurement.* San Diego: Knapp.

Feldman, M. P. 1976. Social psychology and the behaviour therapies. In M. P. Feldman and A. Broadhurst (eds.). *Theoretical and Experimental Bases of the Behaviour Therapies.* London: Wiley.

Feldman, M. P. 1977. *Criminal Behaviour: a Psychological Analysis.* London: Wiley.

Feldman, M. P. 1980. Clinical psychology at Birmingham: the first 100 graduates. *Bulletin of the British Psychological Society*, 33, 85–8.

Feldman, M. P. and Orford, J. F. 1980. *Psychological Problems: The Social Context.* London: J. Wiley.

Fielding, A. G. and Portwood, D. 1980. Professions and the state – towards a typology of bureaucratic professions. *Sociological Review*, 28, 23–53.

Fischer, J. 1978. Does anything work? *Journal of Social Services Research*, 1, 215–43.

Fo, W. S. O. and O'Donnell, C. R. 1975. The buddy system: effect of community intervention on delinquent offences. *Behavior Therapy*, 6, 522–4.

Fodor, I. E. 1972. The use of behaviour modification techniques with female offenders. *Child Welfare*, 51, 93–101.

Foster, B., Gregory, P., Locke, A., Powell, M. and Sutton, A. 1977. *Child Care – A Cause for Concern*, Birmingham: Movement of Practising Psychologists.

Foxen, T. 1978. *Education of the Developmentally Young Mentally Handicapped Child: a Programme of Evaluated Dissemination and Research (Second Report to the DES)* University of Manchester: Hester Adrian Research Centre.

France, R. 1979. Behaviour therapy in general practice. Paper presented to London Branch British Association for Behavioural Psychotherapy.

Francis, J. and Sutton, A. 1977. The battered child and his parents: can we help? *Social Work Today*, 4 January, 16–17.

Freud, S. 1961. *The Complete Psychological Works of Sigmund Freud* (Vol. 19). London: Hogarth.

Frude, N. 1980. *Psychological Perspectives in Child Abuse.* London: Batsfords.

Gagne, R. M. and Briggs, L. J. 1974. *Principles of Instructional Design.* London: Holt Rinehart and Winston.

Gardner, W. I. 1977. *Learning and Behaviour Characteristics of Exceptional Children and Youth: A Humanistic Behavioural Approach.* London: Allyn and Bacon.

Georgiades, N. J. and Phillimore, L. 1975. The myth of the Hero Innovator and alternative strategies for organisational change. In C. Kiernan and F. P. Woodford (eds.). *Behaviour Modification with the Severely Retarded.* Amsterdam: Associated Scientific Publishers.

Ghodsian, M. and Calnan, M. 1977. A comparative longitudinal analysis of special education groups. *British Journal of Educational Psychology*, 47, 162–74.

Gibbons, T. C. N. 1963. *Psychiatric Studies of Borstal Lads.* Oxford: Oxford University Press.

Gillham, W. E. C. 1974. The British Intelligence Scale, à la recherche du temps perdu. *Bulletin of the British Psychological Society*, 27, 307–12.

Gillham, W. (ed.) 1978. *Reconstructing Educational Psychology.* London: Croom Helm.

Glen, F. 1975. *The Social Psychology of Organisations.* London: Methuen.

Glover, E. 1960. *The Roots of Crime.* New York: International Universities Press.

Glueck, S. and Glueck, E. 1956. *Physique and Delinquency.* New York: Harper.

Goldberg, D. P. and Blackwell, B. 1970. Psychiatric illness in general practice. *British Medical Journal*, 2, 439–43.

Graham, H. and Sher, M. 1976. Social work and general practice. *Journal of the Royal College of General Practitioners*, 26, 95–105.

Grant, J. D. and Grant, M. A. 1959. A group dynamics approach to the treatment of non-conformists in the navy. *Annals of the American Academy of Political and Social Science*, 322, 126.

Gray, M. 1979. The myth of objective assessment. *Community Care*, 1 March, 22–3.

Gregory, R. P. 1977. Children in care: a review. In B. Foster, R. P. Gregory, A. Locke, M. Powell and A. Sutton. *Child Care – A Cause for Concern.* Birmingham: Movement of Practising Psychologists, 11–28.

Gregory, R. P. In press. Individual referrals: how naive are educational psychologists. *Bulletin of the British Psychological Society.*

Gregory, R. P. and Tweddle, D. 1978. Planning and evaluating meetings. *Social Work Service*, No. 16, 21–5.

Gregory, R. P. and Tweddle, D. 1979. Teaching independence in community homes. *Social Work Service*, No. 19, 48–52.

Grey, B. 1978. The psychologist working with mentally handicapped adults in the community. In P. Williams (ed.). *Proc. Conf. on the Role of the Psychologist in Social Services Departments.* Wallingford, Oxon, Castle Priory College.

Griffiths, D. 1976. The teaching of psychology in medical schools: A pat on the back or a kick in the pants? *Bulletin of the British*

Psychological Society, **29**, 269–73.

Griffiths, T. 1978. A psychologist's view of psychologist's work. In *Psychology and Primary Care: Proceedings of a Joint Meeting of Northern Region and Scottish DCP Branches.* Leicester: BPS.

Hall, J. N. 1970. Psychological manpower in the Health Service: use or misuse. *Bulletin of the British Psychological Society*, **23**, 219–22.

Hall, S. 1980. *Drifting into a Law and Order Society.* London: Cobden Trust.

Hallam, R. A. and Liddell, A. 1978. A community clinic for teaching psychotherapy. *Bulletin of the British Psychological Society*, **31**, 145–6.

Halsey, A. (ed.) 1972. EPA action research. In *Educational Priority, Vol. 1: EPA Problems and Policies.* London: HMSO.

Hambly, K. and Paxton, R. 1979. The use of behaviour therapy in general practice. *Update*, October, 645–8.

Hargreaves, D. 1978. The proper study of educational psychology. *Journal of the Association of Educational Psychologists*, **49**, 3–8.

Harrop, A. 1974. A behavioural workshop for the management of classroom problems. *British Journal of In-Service Education*, **1**, 47–50.

Hart, D. and Taylor, A. 1979. Publications and educational psychologists. *DECP Occasional Papers*, July.

Hartley, J. and Davies, I. (eds.) 1978. *Contributions to an Educational Technology, Volume 2.* London: Kogan Page.

Hassall, C. and Stillwell, J. A. 1977. Family doctor support for patients on a psychiatric case register. *Journal of the Royal College of General Practitioners*, **27**, 605–8.

Hawks, D. V. 1971. Can clinical psychology afford to treat the individual? *Bulletin of the British Psychological Society*, **24**, 133–5.

Haywood, H. C. 1976. The ethics of doing research . . . and of not doing it. *American Journal of Mental Deficiency*, **81**, 311–17.

Heller, K. and Monahan, J. 1977. *Psychology and Community Change.* Illinois: Dorsey.

Henderson, E. S. 1978. *The Evaluation of In-Service Teacher Training.* London: Croom Helm.

Herbert, M. 1980. Socialisation for problem resistance. In M. P. Feldman and J. F. Orford (eds.). *Psychological Problems: The Social Context.* London: J. Wiley.

Hersen, M. 1976. Token economies in institutional settings. *The Journal of Nervous and Mental Disease*, **162**, 206–11.

Hetherington, R. R. 1967. Psychology in the general hospital. *Bulletin of the British Psychological Society*, **20**, 7–10.

Hodge, H. P. and Bain, L. D. 1971. *Report of a Survey of Secondary Special Schools in Glasgow.* Jordan Hill College of Education.

Hodge, P. 1970. The application of general systems theory of secondary education. In A. J. Romiszowski (ed.). *A Systems Approach to Education and Training* (APELT Occasional Papers No. 1). London: Kogan Page, 72–92.

Hoghughi, M. S., Cumiskey, P. D., McCaffrey, A. and Muckley, A. 1977. *The Franklin Token Economy.* Aycliffe: Aycliffe Studies of Problem Children.

Hoghughi, M. 1978. *Troubled and Troublesome – Coping with Severely Disordered Children.* London: André Deutsch.

Hoghughi, M. 1979a. Myth, method and utility. *Social Work Today*, **10**, 11–13.

Hoghughi, M. 1979b. Towards a more responsible society. *Community Care*, 8 August, 20–2.

Hoghughi, M. 1980a. *Assessing Problem Children: Issues and Practice.* London: André Deutsch.

Hoghughi, M. 1980b. Social work in a bind. *Community Care*, 3 April, 17–23.

Home Office. 1978. *Hostel Study: Report of the Study Conducted in the Midlands during September, 1977.* London: HMSO.

Hood, J. E. 1979. Clinical psychology and primary care: a plea for restraint. *Bulletin of the British Psychological Society*, **32**, 422–3.

Hood, R. and Sparks, R. 1970. *Key Issues in Criminology.* London: Weidenfeld and Nicolson.

Howells, J. G. 1974. *Remember Maria.* London: Butterworths.

Howie, J. 1979. *Research in General Practice.* London: Croom Helm.

Hutchings, J. 1980. The behavioural approach to child abuse: a review of the literature. In N. Frude (ed.). *Psychological Perspectives in Child Abuse.* London: Batsfords.

Hutchings, J. and Jones, D. 1980. Child abuse and parenting skills. *Proc. MIND Ann. Conf. (London, 1979).* London: MIND.

Hyman, I. and Schrieber, K. 1975. Selected concepts and practices of child advocacy in school psychology. *Psychology in the Schools*, **12**, 50–8.

Ingham, J. and Miller, P. 1979. Symptom prevalence and severity in a general practice population. *Journal of Epidemiology and Community Health*, **33**, 191–8.

Ingleby, D. 1975. The psychology of child psychology. In M. P. M. Richards (ed.). *Integration of the Child into a Social World.* London: Cambridge Univ. Press.

Irvine, D. 1979. Education for general practice. In J. Fry (ed.). *Trends in General Practice 1979.* London: RCGP.

Ives, G. 1979. Psychological treatment in general practice. *Journal of the Royal College of General Practitioners*, **29**, 348–51.

Jarvik, L. F., Klodin, V. and Matsuyama, S. S. 1973. Human aggression and the extra Y chromosome: Fact or fantasy. *American Psychologist*, **28**, 674–83.

Jeffery, C. R. 1965. Criminal behaviour and learning theory. *The Journal of Criminal Law, Criminology and Police Science*, **56**, 294–300.

Jenkin, P. 1980. Speech to House of Commons, 23 January.

Jesness, C. F. 1974. Comparative effectiveness of behaviour modification and transactional analysis programs for delinquents. *Journal of Consulting and Clinical Psychology*, **6**, 758–79.

Johnson, V. S. 1977. Behavior modification in the correctional setting. *Criminal Justice and Behavior*, **4**, 397–428.

Johnston, M. 1978. The work of a clinical psychologist in primary care. *Journal of the Royal College of General Practitioners*, **28**, 661–7.

Jordan, B. 1974. *Poor Parents: Social Policy and the 'Cycle of Deprivation'.* London: Routledge and Kegan Paul.

Joseph, K. 1972. Speech to the preschool playgroups association, 29 June.

Kat, B. 1978. Primary health care: on finding one's place in the team. *Bulletin of the British Psychological Society*, **31**, 154–6.

Kat, B. 1980a. Working party on manpower planning: Exponential growth – but how long can it last? *Division of Clinical Psychology Newsletter*, **27**, 6–9.

Kat, B. 1980b. Prevention and the psychology of primary health care. Paper presented at the British Psychological Society Annual Conference, Aberdeen.

Katz, D. and Kahn, R. L. 1978. *The Social Psychology of Organisations.* NY: Wiley.

Kear-Colwell, J. 1972. A study of clinical psychologists' job movements during the period 1 October 1967 – 30 September 1970. *Bulletin of the British Psychological Society*, **25**, 25–7.

Keir, G. 1952. A history of child-guidance. *British Journal of Educational Psychology*, **22**, 12–29.

Kelly, J. G. (ed.) 1979. *Adolescent Boys in High School: A Psychological Study of Coping and Adaptation.* New Jersey: Lawrence Erlbaum Assoc.

Kincey, J. A. 1974. General practice and clinical psychology – some arguments for a closer liaison. *Journal of the Royal College of General Practitioners*, 24, 882–8.

King, M. 1976. *Roles and Relationships in the Magistrates' Courts.* Birmingham: Movement of Practising Psychologists, Discussion Paper No. 9.

Koch, H. 1979. Evaluation of behaviour therapy intervention in general practice. *Journal of the Royal College of General Practitioners*, 29, 337–40.

Krasner, L. (ed.). In press. *Experimental Design and Human Behaviour: A Handbook of Theory and Application.* Elmsford, NY: Pergamon.

Laishley, J. and Coleman, J. 1978a. Community psychology for the under fives. *Bulletin of the British Psychological Society*, 31, 227–8.

Laishley, J. and Coleman, J. 1978b. Action research in day nurseries: evaluation programmes through staff perceptions and attitudes. *Child: Care, Health and Development*, 4, 159–69.

Levitt, E. E. 1957. The results of psychotherapy with children: an evaluation. *Journal of Consulting Psychology*, 21, 189–96.

Ley, P. and Spellman, M. S. 1967. *Communicating With the Patient.* London: Staples Press.

Lickorish, J. R. and Sims, C. A. 1971. How much can a clinical psychologist do? *Bulletin of the British Psychological Society*, 24, 27–30.

Logan, C. H. 1972. Evaluation research in crime and delinquency: a reappraisal. *Journal of Criminal Law, Criminology and Police Science*, 63, 378–87.

Lombroso, C. 1911. *Crime, its Causes and Remedies.* Boston: Little, Brown.

Loxley, D. 1976. *The Child Sterilisation Case: Some Background Issues.* Birmingham: Movement of Practising Psychologists (Pamphlet No. 8).

Loxley, D. 1978. Community psychology. In W. Gillham (ed.). *Reconstructing Educational Psychology.* London: Croom Helm.

Luriya, A. R. 1979. *The Making of a Mind.* Cambridge, Mass.: Harvard University Press.

Luthans, F. and Kreitner, R. 1975. *Organisational Behaviour Modification.* Glenview, Illinois: Scott Foresmann.

McAllister, T. and Philip, A. E. 1975. The clinical psychologist in a health centre: one year's work. *British Medical Journal*, 4, 513–14.

McCaffrey, L. and Cummings, J. In H. Dupont (ed.) 1969. *Educating Educationally Disturbed Children.* NY: Holt Rinehart Winston.

McCartney, J. B. and O'Mahoney, D. S. 1977. The legal responsibilities of psychologists. *Bulletin of the British Psychological Society*, **30**, 378–9.

McEwan, P. (Chmn.). 1978. Report of the Working Party on abuses of psychology. *Bulletin of the British Psychological Society*, **31**, 95.

McGuire, W. J. 1980. Communication and social influence processes. In M. P. Feldman and J. F. Orford (eds.). *Psychological Probelms: The Social Context.* London: J. Wiley.

McPherson, I. G. 1980. Clinical psychology in primary care – another case of innovation without change? Paper presented at the British Psychological Society Annual Conference, Aberdeen.

McPherson, I. G. and Feldman, M. P. 1977. A preliminary investigation of the role of the clinical psychologist in the primary care setting. *Bulletin of the British Psychological Society*, **30**, 342–6.

Manpower Services Commission. 1979. *The Relevance and Application of the MSC Special Programmes for the Unemployed to Ex-offenders and those Non-offenders 'At Risk'.* London: New Opportunity Press.

Marks, I. M. 1970. Epidemiology of phobic disorders. *British Journal of Social Psychiatry*, **4**, 109–14.

Marks, I. M. 1973. Research in neurosis: a selective review. 1. Causes and courses. *Psychological Medicine*, **3**, 436–54.

Marks, J. 1978. *The Benzodiazepines: Use, Overuse, Misuse, Abuse.* Lancaster: MTP.

Matthews, C. F. 1975. The relationship between reading skills and IQ in an assessment centre sample. *Community Home Schools Gaz.*, **68**, 617–18.

Mays, J. B. 1963. *Crime and the Social Structure.* London: Faber.

Meacher, M. 1976. *A pilot Counselling Scheme with General Practitioners.* London: Mental Health Foundation.

Medway, F. J. 1975. A social psychological approach to internally-based change in schools. *Journal of School Psychology*, **13**, 19–27.

Midwinter, E. 1977. The professional–lay relationship: a Victorian legacy. *Journal of Child Psychology and Psychiatry*, **18**, 101–13.

Milan, M. A., Wood, L. F., Williams, R. L., Rogers, J. G., Hampton, L. R. and McKee, J. M. 1974. *Applied Behavioural Analysis and the Imprisoned Adult Felon. Project 1: the Cellblock Token Economy.* Montgomery, Al: Rehabilitation Research Foundation.

Miller, E. 1968. A case for automated clinical testing. *Bulletin of the British Psychological Society*, **21**, 75–8.

Miller, G. A. 1969. Psychology as a means of promoting human welfare. *American Psychologist*, 24, 1063–75.

Mischel, W. 1976. *Introduction to Personality*. New York: Rinehart and Winston.

Mishler, E. G. and Waxler, E. G. 1963. Decision processes in psychiatric hospitalisation: patients referred, accepted and admitted to psychiatric hospitals. *American Sociological Review*, 28, 576.

Mitford, J. 1973. *Kind and Unusual Punishment*. New York: Knopf.

Morgan, P. 1975. *Child Care, Sense and Fable*. London: Temple Smith.

Morgan, P. 1978. *Delinquent Fantasies*. London: Temple Smith.

Morris, L. L. and Fitzgibbon, C. T. 1978. *Program Evaluation Kit: Evaluator's Handbook*. London: Sage Publications.

Moss, G. and Sutton, A. 1980. Educational Psychologists and the Juvenile Court. In *Law and Psychology*. Oxford: Centre for Socio-legal Studies.

Mulhall, D. 1980. In press. Not enough service in the national health. *Bulletin of the British Psychological Society*.

Munro, R. G. 1977. *Innovation: Success or Failure*. London: Hodder and Stoughton.

Nelson, E. K., Ohmart, H. and Barlow, N. 1979. *Promising Strategies in Probation and Parole*. LEAA Report, Washington, DC: US Government Printing Office.

Neville, C. 1978. Developing strategies for in-service training in educational technology. In D. Brook and P. Race (eds.). *Aspects of Educational Technology, Vol. XII Education Technology in Changing World*. London: Kogan Page.

Newson, J. and Newson, E. 1968. *Four-Years Old in an Urban Community*. London: Allen and Unwin.

Nietzel, M. T. 1979. *Crime and its Modification. A Social Learning Perspective*. New York: Pergamon, General Psychology Series.

Norris, A. 1978. Principals' principles. *Newsletter*, West Midlands Branch, Division of Clinical Psychology. 11, 2–4.

O'Donnell, C. 1980. Environmental design and the prevention of psychological problems. In M. P. Feldman and J. F. Orford (eds.). *Psychological Problems: The Social Context*. London: J. Wiley.

Olweus, D. 1975. Bullies and whipping boys. In J. deWit and W. W. Hartup (eds.). *Determinants and Origins of Aggressive Behaviour*. The Hague: Mouton.

Orford, J. 1979. Teaching community psychology to undergraduate and postgraduate psychology students. *Bulletin of the British Psychological Society*, 32, 75–9.

Ostapiuk, E. B. 1977. Behaviour and attitude change following institutional and community based treatment programmes for delinquents. Unpublished MSc thesis, University of Birmingham.

Ostapiuk, E. B., Morrison, N. and Porteus, M. A. 1976. A brief numerical summary of some family variables among boys in an assessment centre. *Community Home Schools Gaz.*, 67, 571–80.

Ostapiuk, E. B. and Reid, I. D. In press. Teaching delinquents survival skills in the community. *Learning.*

Parry, N. and Parry, J. 1979. Social work, professionalism and the state. In N. Parry, M. Rustin and C. Satyamurti (eds.). *Social Work, Welfare and the State.* London: Arnold, 21–47.

Peck, D. 1978. Communications and compliance. *Bulletin of the British Psychological Society*, 31, 348–52.

Peck, D. F. and Gathercole, C. E. 1968. Automation techniques in clinical psychology. *Bulletin of the British Psychological Society*, 21, 161–5.

Pendelton, D., Schofield, T. and Furnham, A. 1978. Social psychology and medical practice. *Bulletin of the British Psychological Society*, 31, 386–7.

Pendelton, D. and Tate, P. 1980. Research and training in the skills of communication between G.P. and patient. Paper presented at the British Psychological Society Annual Conference, Aberdeen.

Phillips, E. L. 1968. Achievement Place: token reinforcement procedures in a home style rehabilitation setting for some delinquent boys. *Journal of Applied Behaviour Analysis*, 1, 213–23.

Piaget, J. 1932. *The Moral Judgment of the Child.* London: Routledge and Kegan Paul.

Pivan, F; F. and Cloward, R. A. 1972. *Regulating the Poor.* London: Tavistock.

Porteous, M. A. 1979. Psychologists in social services: alternative tasks. In P. Williams (ed.). *Proc. Conf. on the Role of Psychologists in Social Services Departments.* Wallingford, Oxon, Castle Priory College.

Presland, J. 1970. Who should go to ESN schools? *Special Education*, 59, 11–16.

Presland, J. 1978. Modifying behaviour in ordinary classrooms. *Association for Behaviour Modification with Children Newsletter*, 2, 15–19.

Pritchard, P. 1978. *Manual of Primary Health Care.* Oxford: OUP.

Project New Pride: an Exemplary Project. LEAA Report, Washington, DC: Office of Juvenile Justice and Delinquency Prevention.

Pumfrey, P. D. and Ward, J. 1971. A four-year follow-up study of maladjusted and normal children, *Bulletin of the British Psychological Society*, 24, 155.

Quicke, J. 1978. The professional knowledge of educational psychologists. *Journal of the Association of Educational Psychologists*, 4, 8–16.

Rachman, S. J. 1972. *The Effects of Psychotherapy*. Oxford: Pergamon.

Rappaport, J. 1977. *Community Psychology*. New York: Holt, Rinehart and Winston.

Raven, J. 1975. Social research in modern society. *Administration*, 23, 225–68.

RCA. 1977. Survey on training. *Residential Social Work*, May.

Reavley, W. and Gilbert, M. T. 1978. The behavioural treatment approach to potential child abuse – two illustrative cases. *Social Work Today*, 7, 166–8.

Reedy, B. 1979. The health team. In J. Fry (ed.). *Trends in General Practice, 1979*. London: RCGP.

Reid, I. D., Feldman, M. P. and Ostapiuk, E. 1980. The Shape Project for young offenders: introduction and overview. *Journal of Offender Counselling Services and Rehabilitation*, 4, 233–46.

Reid, I. D. and Ostapiuk, E. B. 1979. Developing a behavioural regime in a secure youth treatment centre. Unpublished Manuscript, Glenthorne Youth Treatment Centre.

Reid, S. T. 1976. *Crime and Criminology*. Hinsdale, Illinois: Dryden Press.

Report of the Industrial Tribunal, Case No. 23995/77, Corina vs Berkshire County Council. 1978. Unpublished.

Repucci, N. D. and Saunders, J. T. 1974. Social psychology of behaviour modification: problems of implementation in natural settings. *American Psychologist*, 9, 649–60.

Reynolds, D. and Murgatroyd, S. J. 1977. The sociology of schooling and the absent pupil: the school as a factor in the generation of truancy. In H. C. M. Carroll (ed.). *Absenteeism in South Wales: Studies of Pupils, their Homes and their Secondary Schools*. Swansea: Faculty of Education.

Robertson, N. C. 1979. Variations in referral pattern to the psychiatric services by general practitioners. *Psychological Medicine*, 9, 355–64.

Robinson, P. 1978. A study of the stresses reported by managers. Unpublished MSc Project, Department of Psychology, University of Birmingham.

Roe, M. A. 1965. *A Survey into Progress of Maladjusted Pupils*. London: ILEA.

Romiszowski, A. J. (ed.) 1970. *A Systems Approach to Education and*

Training (APLET Occasional Papers No. 1). London: Kogan Page.

Rutter, M. 1972. *Maternal Deprivation Reassessed.* Harmondsworth: Penguin Books.

Rutter, M. and Madge, M. 1976. *Cycles of Disadvantage.* London: Heinemann.

Rutter, M., Maughan, B., Mortimore, P. and Ouston, J. 1979. *Fifteen Thousand Hours: Secondary Schools and their effects on Children.* London: Open Books.

Rutter, M., Tizard, J. and Whitmore, K. (eds.) 1970. *Education, Health and Behaviour.* London: Longmans.

Sage, W. 1974. Crime and the clockwork lemon. *Human Behaviour,* 9, 16–25.

Sawyer, C. E. and Brown, B. J. 1977. Laterality and intelligence in relation to reading ability. *Educational Review,* 29, 81–6.

SCANUS. 1976. *Social Work and the Welfare State.* London: SCANUS.

Scheff, T. J. 1966. *Being Mentally Ill: a Sociological Theory.* London: Weidenfeld and Nicolson.

Schur, E. M. 1965. *Crimes without Victims: Deviant Behaviour and Public Policy: Abortion, Homosexuality, Drug Addiction.* Englewood Cliffs, New Jersey: Prentice-Hall.

Schwitzgebel, R. 1964. *Street Corner Research: an Experimental Approach to Juvenile Delinquents.* Cambridge, Massachusetts: Harvard University Press.

Seebohm Report (Cmnd. No. 3703) 1968. *Report of the Committee on Local Authority and Allied Personal Services.* London: HMSO.

Shackleton-Bailey, M. J. 1979. Psychologists and the personal social services. In P. Williams (ed.). *Proc. Conf. on the Role of the Psychologist in the Social Services.* Wallingford, Oxon, Castle Priory College.

Shapiro, D., Parry, G. and Brewin, C. 1979. Stress, coping and psychotherapy: the foundations of a clinical approach. In T. Cox and C. Mackay (eds.). *Response to Stress: Occupational Aspects.* London: IPC.

Sheldon, B. 1980. Psychology and social work. In M. Brown and L. Muir (eds.). *Social Work Practice: a Basic Text.* London: McDonald.

Sheldon, W. H. 1942. *The Varieties of Temperament: A Psychology of Constitutional Differences.* New York: Harper and Brothers.

Shepherd, M., Cooper, B., Brown, A. and Katton, G. 1966. *Psychiatric Illness in General Practice.* London: OUP.

Shepherd, M., Oppenheim, A. N. and Mitchell, S. 1966. Childhood behaviour disorders and the child guidance clinic: an epidemiological study. *Journal of Child Psychology and Psychiatry*, 7, 39–52.

Shulman, L. S. 1970. Reconstruction of educational research. *Review of Educational Research*, **40**, 371–96.

Smith, S. M., Hanson, R. and Noble, S. 1973. Parents of battered babies, a controlled study. *British Medical Journal*, No. 4, 338–91.

Spencer, N. 1979. Doctors and the acquisition of clients' health knowledge. In D. Anderson (ed.). *Health Education in Practice*. London: Croom Helm.

Srole, L., Langer, T. S., Michael, S. T., Oflar, M. K. and Rennie, T. A. C. 1962. *Mental Health in the Metropolis: the midtown Manhattan study*, volume 1. New York: McGraw-Hill Book Company.

SSRC. 1980. *Children in Need of Care*. London: Social Sciences Research Council, 8–16.

Start unconstitutional. 1974. *APA Monitor*, **5**, 12–13.

Stenhouse, L. 1975. *An Introduction to Curriculum Research and Development*. London: Heinemann.

Stufflebeam, D. L. 1968. Towards a Science of Educational Evaluation. *Educational Technology*, July 30, 5–12.

Stufflebeam, D. L., Foley, W. J., Gephart, W. J., Guba, E. G., Hammond, R. L., Merriman, H. O. and Provus, M. M. 1971. *Educational Evaluation Decision Making*. Itasca, Illinois: Peacock.

Stumphauzer, J. S. 1970. Behaviour modification with juvenile delinquents: a critical review. *Federal Correctional Institution Technical and Treatment Notes*, **1**, 1–22.

Stumphauzer, J. S. 1973. *Behaviour Therapy with Delinquents*. Springfield, Illinois: Thomas.

Suedefield, P. 1979. Abuses of psychology for political purposes (letter). *Bulletin of the British Psychological Society*, **32**, 431.

Sutton, A. 1976. Child psychology and local government, *Journal of the Association of Educational Psychologists*, **4**, 9–14.

Sutton, A. 1977. Advocacy: the psychologist as an agent for social change. *Journal of the Association of Educational Psychologists*, **4**, 12–15.

Sutton, A. 1978a. The psychologist's professionalism and the right to psychology. In W. Gillham (ed.). *Reconstructing Educational Psychology*. London: Croom Helm, 144–60.

Sutton, A. 1978b. Theory, practice and cost in child care: implications from an individual case. *Howard Journal of Penology and Crime Prevention*, **16**, 159–71.

Sutton, A. 1978c. Reports to the juvenile court – rituals or revelations? *Legal Action Group Bulletin*, July, 155–57.

Sutton, A. 1981. Science in court. In M. King (ed.). *Childhood, Welfare and Justice.* London: Batsfords.

Sutton, A. 1980a. Sorting the wheat from the chaff: the examination of expert evidence on child care matters. In *Reports for the Courts.* London: Family Rights Group.

Sutton, A. 1980b. Child abuse procedures – are they worth the risk? *Legal Action Group Bulletin*, May.

Sutton, A. and Collins, S. 1977. Day care and the problems of deprivation and disadvantage. In *The Handicapped Preschool Child.* London: British Psychological Society (Division of Educational and Child Psychology), 21–38.

Sutton, C. 1979. *Psychology for Social Workers and Counsellors: an Introduction.* London: Routledge and Kegan Paul.

Tapp, J., Krull, R., Tapp, M. and Seller, R. H. 1978. The application of behavior modification to behavior management: Guidelines for the family physician. *Journal of Family Practice*, 6, 293–9.

Taylor, G. 1978. A G.P.'s view of psychologist's work. In *Psychology and Primary Care: Proceedings of a joint meeting of Northern Region and Scottish D.C.P. Branches.* Leicester: BPS.

Teare, P. and Brown, B. J. 1977. Gilbey House, six months on. *Community Home Schools Gaz.*, 71, 188–92.

Temperley, J. 1978. Psychotherapy in the setting of general medical practice. *British Journal of Medical Psychology*, 51, 139–45.

Teuber, N. and Powers, E. 1953. Evaluating therapy in a delinquency prevention programme. *Proceedings of the Association for Research in Nervous and Mental Diseases*, 3, 138.

Tharp, R. G. and Wetzel, R. H. 1969. *Behaviour Modification in the Natural Environment.* New York: Academic Press.

Tizard, B. 1977. *Adoption: a Second Chance.* London: Open Books.

Tizard, J. 1973. Maladjusted children and the child guidance service. *London Educational Review*, 2, 22–37.

Todd, A. R. 1968. *Report of the Royal Commission on Medical Education, 1965–1968.* London: HMSO.

Topping, K. 1977. Investigation of aspects of the role and functioning of a city psychological service. Unpublished Dissertation, Department of Psychology, University of Nottingham.

Topping, K. 1979. Consumer confusion in school psychology. *Bulletin of the British Psychological Society*, 32, 211.

Town, S. W. 1973. Action research and social policy: some recent British experience. *Sociological Review*, 21, 573–98.

Townsend, P. and Abel-Smith, B. 1965. *The Poor and the Poorest.* London: Bell.

Trethowan, W. H. 1977. *The Role of Psychologists in the Health Service.* London: HMSO.

Trotter, S. 1974. ACLU scores token economy. *APA Monitor*, 5, 36–41.

Trotter, S. 1975. Token economy program perverted by prison officials. *APA Monitor*, 6, 24–7.

Tully, B., Doyle, M., Cahill, D., Bayles, T. and Graham, D. 1978. Psychology and community work in mental health. *Bulletin of the British Psychological Society*, 31, 115–19.

Tutt, N. (ed.). 1974. *Care or Custody: Community Homes and the Treatment of Delinquency.* London: Darton, Longman and Todd.

Tutt, N. 1979. *Short, Sharp Shocks – There Must be an Alternative!* London: Justice for Children, Pamphlet No. 15.

Tutt, N. and Tutt, C. 1975. So you think you know better . . . *Community Care*, 20 August, 20–1.

Tyerman, M. J. 1975. Psychologists and team work. *Journal of the Association of Educational Psychologists*, 3, 16–20.

US Bureau of the Census. 1979. *Children in Custody: Advance Report on the 1977 Census of Public Juvenile Facilities* Washington, DC: US Government Printing Office.

Vacc, N. A. 1972. Longterm effect of special class intervention for emotionally disturbed children. *Exceptional Children*, 39, 15–23.

Vernon, P. E. 1968. What is potential ability? *Bulletin of the British Psychological Society*, 21, 211–19.

Wales, E. 1978. Behavioural scientist meets the practising physician. *Journal of Family Practice*, 6, 839–44.

Walker, N. 1965. *Crime and Punishment in Britain.* Edinburgh: University Press.

Walker, N. 1967. *Crimes, Courts and Figures: an Introduction to Criminal Statistics.* London: Pelican.

Warnock Report (Cmnd 7212). 1978. *Report of the Committee of Enquiry into the Education of Handicapped Children and Young People.* London: HMSO.

Warren, M. Q., Palmer, T. B., Neto, V. and Turner, K. 1966. *Community Treatment Project: Research Report No. 7.* Sacramento, California: California Youth and Adult Correction Authority.

Watson, L. 1972. *How to Use Behaviour Modification with Mentally Retarded and Autistic Children: Programs for Administrators, Teachers, Parents and Nurses.* Illinois: Behaviour Modification Technology.

Waydenfield, D. and Waydenfield, S. 1979. *Counselling in the General*

Practice Setting. London: Marriage Guidance Council.

Webb, B. 1948. *Our Partnership.* London: Longmans.

Wedell, K. and Lambourne, R. 1979. *An Enquiry into Psychological Services for Children in England and Wales.* Birmingham: Faculty of Education.

Weinmann, J. 1978. Integrating psychology with general medicine. *Bulletin of the British Psychological Society*, 31, 352–5.

Wetzel, R. 1966. Use of behavioural techniques in a case of compulsive stealing. *Journal of Consulting Psychology*, 30, 367–74.

Wheelan, E. and Speake, B. 1977. *Adult Training Centres in England and Wales.* London: NATMH.

White, J. G. 1972. What is wrong with clinical psychology? *Bulletin of the British Psychological Society*, 25, 101–6.

Whittaker, E. M. 1977. Aspects of intellectual and educational functioning of boys admitted to the regional assessment centre. *Journal of the Association of Educational Psychologists*, 4, 24–30.

Williams, P. (ed.) 1979. *Proc. Conf. on the Role of the Psychologist in the Social Services.* Wallingford, Oxon, Castle Priory College.

Williams, R. 1980. The fate of Maudsley psychologists – a survey of recent students. *Bulletin of the British Psychological Society*, 33, 82–4.

Windle, C., Bass, R. D. and Taube, C. A. 1974. P. R. aside: initial results from N.I.M.H's service program evaluation studies. *American Journal of Community Psychology*, 2, 311–17.

Wing, J. K. and Hailey, A. M. 1972. *Evaluating a Community Psychiatric Service.* London: Oxford University Press.

Winter, R. D. and Whitfield, M. J. 1980. General practitioners, counselling and psychotherapy. *Update*, March, 637–47.

Wolfe, R. W. and Marino, D. 1975. A programme of behaviour treatment for incarcerated pedophiles. *The American Criminal Law Review*, 1, 69–83.

Wright, J. 1974. Reporting findings. In M. Chazan (ed.). *The Practice of Educational Psychology.* London: Longman, 257–79.

Yates, A. 1975. *The Theory and Practice of Behavior Therapy.* New York: Wiley.

Yule, W. and Raynes, R. D. 1972. The behavioural characteristics of children in residential care in relation to indices of separation. *Journal of Child Psychology and Psychiatry*, 13, 249–58.

Zeeman, C. 1976. Catastrophe theory. *Scientific American*, 234, 65–83.

CONTRIBUTORS

Barrie Brown Senior Lecturer in Psychology, Institute of Psychiatry, London.

Robert Burden Lecturer in Educational Psychology, University of Exeter.

Philip Feldman Reader in Clinical Psychology, University of Birmingham.

R. Paul Gregory Educational Psychologist, Sutton Coldfield.

David Hawks Top Grade Clinical Psychologist, South Glamorgan AHA; Hon. Professor, UWIST; Consultant Adviser in Clinical Psychology to DHSS.

Ian McPherson Lecturer in Clinical Psychology, University of Birmingham.

Eugene Ostapiuk Senior Psychologist, Glenthorne Youth Treatment Centre, Birmingham (formerly Programme Director, Shape).

Ian Reid Programme Director, Glenthorne Youth Treatment Centre, Birmingham.

Andrew Sutton Psychologist, Birmingham LEA and Parent and Child Centre (Birmingham AHA and Social Services Department); Hon. Lecturer, University of Birmingham.

INDEX

202 *Index*